WHEN THE WOOD IS GREEN

Arthur Fay Sueltz

WHEN THE WOOD IS GREEN

1817 HARPER & ROW, PUBLISHERS
New York • Evanston • San Francisco • London

 For information address Harper & Row, Publishers, Inc., 10 East 53rd Street, New York, N.Y. 10022. Published simultaneously in Canada by Fitzhenry & Whiteside Limited, Toronto.

FIRST EDITION

Designed by C. Linda Dingler

Library of Congress Cataloging in Publication Data

Sueltz, Arthur Fay
When the wood is green.
Includes bibliographical references.
1. Christian life—1960– I. Title.
BV4501.2.S83 1973 248'.4 73–6346
ISBN 0–06–067759–7

CONTENTS

PREFACE

A few years ago I had an inner crisis that scared the hell out of me. Literally. Somewhere in our thirties or early forties a lot of us feel like life has us by the throat. We find ourselves facing all kinds of new personal issues. All at once I saw that I would have to begin unlearning a lot of what people had told me about myself and God and the world. Not everything, of course. But I had learned things that tied me up in knots and left me standing on the edge of the abyss. Suddenly I began to see that some of what I'd been taught made God sound incredible and hard to believe. Yet I went right on believing! Caught in that tension I looked for help.

I'd been taught to pray, but I had to quit because suddenly my praying felt like a parade of trite religious jargon. I could pray up a storm in a religious setting while secretly wondering what the people listening thought of my prayer. Suddenly I saw that that wasn't praying: that was hell. And I found that about all I could say in hell was, "Oh God, help me!" Probably the most direct honest contact I'd tried to make with God in years.

I needed all kinds of help. So I began looking for people who could help me think through some of the issues involved in my time of agonizing reappraisal. God can't be reduced to an idea or a thought process: still there's truth in the statement that as a man thinketh in his heart, so he is. I began to get in touch with my own feelings and become sensitive to the feelings of others. And I began taking some of the risks involved in making myself as vulnerable and as open to God and to people as I could. But beyond all that I also felt that I needed to get my religious thinking out of a dream world and in touch with reality. If I had begun to relate with new honesty to God I had also to begin thinking honestly about Him. I began developing a new sensitivity to spiritual values. As Blaise Pascal said, "The heart has its reasons which reason does not know."

All kinds of people have helped me to do it. Personal friends and writers both religious and secular. Many of their ideas, words, and phrases have stuck in my mind and heart in ways I cannot dislodge. Today when I speak, their words often come out as my own, as in fact they have become. I feel somehow "bound up in the bundle of life with them." And many of these contributors to my new life don't even know the immense contributions they've made. I know many of them through the printed page, and they don't know me at all. Those who helped the most shared their own personal thought processes in ways I could identify with. People like David H. C. Read, Theodore Parker Ferris, William Barker, John A. Mackay and a whole host of others too numerous to mention. Whatever is good in this book they and men like them helped me learn. The rest I did on my own.

Then one summer while camping in Yosemite National Park I read Luke's account of Jesus on the way to the cross. Luke implies that some women along the way said in effect, "This shouldn't happen to a man like this." And according to the Gospel writer, Jesus answered, "If they do this when the wood is green, what will happen when it is dry?" I couldn't get that phrase "when the wood is green . . ." out of my mind. What did Jesus mean? I looked it up in all the commentaries I could lay my hands on, but they didn't help much. The phrase seems to defy adequate explanation. Perhaps that's just as well. In my experience God often works like that, in ways that defy precise explanation. Still, Jesus meant something when he used the phrase. For me he raised the issue of how many commonly accepted values in life actually run against the grain of God's creation. If that happened in the experience of Jesus, then his experience certainly checks out with mine—hence the title of this book.

Long Beach, California ARTHUR Fay SUELTZ

WHEN THE WOOD IS GREEN

1. WHEN FAMILIAR LANDMARKS DISAPPEAR

When familiar landmarks disappear, what then?

A vital young man stands by the window in his office. His wife lies in the hospital where she has been for several months. A few weeks earlier his company has hired an attractive young woman, with whom he has had several "business luncheons." He can feel something starting between them. Today they are to have another meeting, and he has arranged it for dinner. As he walks back to his desk he asks himself, "What would happen if I went to Marie's apartment after dinner? Suppose I stayed overnight in town just this once? Who would know? After all, why should I try to suppress my legitimate appetites? I need the love and affection of a woman. Why should I let Eleanor's condition frustrate me?"

What does one need besides the satisfaction of one's appetites in order to lead a fully human life? "I want to live, live out, not wobble through my life somehow and then into the dark."[1] But how can I get my bearings? When familiar landmarks disappear, what can I use as a point of reference? Once, perhaps, men believed they knew what was right even if they chose not to do it. But today it's not so much a problem of doing what I know is right; now it's a matter of knowing what's right. The conflicting testimony I hear suggests that the question is not so much one of expertise as of outlook. So my search for some towering point of reference grows acute. What can help me see the difference between what's possible and what's desirable? Such insight demands not only accurate information but also an adequate understanding of the data. I want to see through the superficial to the essential.

The Old Testament describes the early experience of a group of people pushing into an unknown land. They had no reliable maps, and no one knew the territory. All the familiar landmarks lay behind them. Soon they began to feel unsettled. They could get lost in this uncharted world. And someone came up with a daring plan: "Let's build a tower so high that its top will reach the heavens, or we'll be scattered over the face of the earth." These people, too, felt the need of some high point of reference, so they built the Tower of Babel. Yes, no doubt their architectural fantasies grew out of inflated human pride. Yet haven't we all dreamed of finding somewhere a lofty point from which we could get our bearings? Some tower reaching to the heavens——

And suddenly I sense that when we start talking about that kind of landmark, we're talking God. Maybe there's more to religion than meets the eye. But how does one work out a viable, responsible way of life, sensitive to the changing issues of our time, alert to the timelessness of the gospel of Jesus Christ, and aware of one's own deep human needs? A lot of us remember going through painful religious crises as we grew and struggled for maturity. Some of us rejected the religious certainties of our parents and in the process nearly lost hold on faith altogether. It wasn't always easy to see that God and ideas about God are not necessarily the same. So often when I rejected an inadequate idea about God, I felt as if I had rejected God Himself. Yet some of us went through times when we had to make a clear break with what lay behind and step out into a new and unknown way. And often that's the best thing to do with religious landmarks I've known in the past. Leave them behind. They no longer adequately mark our present geography. The new wine will burst the old wineskins.

I remember singing hymns like "Safe in the Arms of Jesus" and feeling a warm sentimental glow. As though the presence of God simply meant warm religious feelings. It's a good thing to leave a lot of that behind. The trouble is that in the process I can lose my sense of God's real presence as a personal companion and guide.

At one time I remember I was forever taking my own spiritual temperature. How often had I read the Bible? A kind of religious good work—no wonder we got rid of it! But sometimes when we did we also left behind any interest in a uniquely Christian quality and style of living. Someone has commented that we used to sing, "Earthly pleasures vainly call me—I would be like Jesus"; now we've updated it to go, "TV, sex, and ease enthrall me—who ever heard of Jesus?"

And sometimes faith in God meant withdrawal from this

world: a retreat as real as that of any monk who ever withdrew into a monastery in the Middle Ages. Faith turned into a negative event. Avoid contamination. A real Christian did not smoke, or drink, or dance, or use lipstick, or go to the movies. The list of specifics varied. In some areas movies were all right, but mixed bathing was wicked. The point always remained the same: withdraw. Faith in God meant something strictly private and inner and unspotted by the world.

At the same time others seemed to confuse faith in God with the confirmation of our particular American way of life. To be a good Christian simply meant being a good American. Yet a lot of us remember how that kind of label led to horrible extremes in Germany of the late 1930s, when a national church gave moral support, but not guidance, to the state. To be a good Christian simply meant being a good German. Strange how my values, the signs from which I take direction in life, often reflect little more than my social environment. An American may see a close connection between God and capitalism, but a deeply committed Christian in Prague may see just as easy and close a connection between God and a cooperative economy or socialism.

So a lot of us all over the world have begun to leave many venerable religious sign posts behind. But now, with old landmarks disappearing, we long for the inner freedom to be and to know. Suddenly Jesus himself looms on the horizon. Not long ago, two young Englishmen wrote and recorded a rock opera celebrating the suffering and crucifixion of Jesus. In seven months *Jesus Christ Superstar* hit the top of the charts from Thailand to Brazil. I even heard it coming over the loudspeakers as background music for the warm-up before a University of California vs. Stanford basketball game. When a pickup group of artists performed the opera for seventy-five hundred people in Kansas City, the audience sang along and at the end cheered and gave a standing ovation.

Maybe there's something in the wind. A lot of our children seem to have felt God's absence long enough. Perhaps the Christian faith does offer resources for the fulfillment of personal and corporate life. Jesus seems to have lived at a time when religion had become formal, clubbish, and dead. Ritual had replaced vitality. Worship often only echoed the past values of the culture. Attendance at synagogue had gone dramatically down. God seemed distant and unreal. Then Jesus came. Men began to sense a living God in the struggle between their faith and their doubt. As Jesus exposed himself, they could see God alive in the tension between their thinking and their feeling. A sight like that's worth several worship services filled with ancient hymns and archaic creeds.

Suppose in this Jesus I begin to rediscover that high tower for which I've been looking. What kind of direction will I get from him? I don't need lofty moral ideals to increase my sense of guilt; I have plenty of guilt already. Yet suddenly I hear Jesus saying, "Don't think I have come to do away with the law of Moses and the teaching of the prophets. I have not come to do away with them but to give them real meaning."

So my mind goes back to that mob of liberated slaves who came out of Egypt. They too had left their old familiar landmarks behind and started out into the unknown. Suppose God wanted to help these people develop a new sense of personal destiny, a new sense of community, a new sense of purpose. Could any of this happen if everybody simply did his own thing? Could God provide any new guidance they could use in the affirmation of their lives?

One day Moses disappeared from camp. He showed up later with two stone tablets. "Word," he said, "direct from God." Word from God, who loved people and worried about the hazards of living on this planet. Gracious words warning people about where those hazards are. Words like "Don't kill." "Don't steal." "Don't commit adultery." "Don't lie." As though killing and stealing, adultery and lying constitute deadly perils to human dignity, human community, and human destiny. On these rocks a man or a people can shatter life-giving relationships. It looks as if God cared enough about how my life turns out to give me guidance that will serve its fulfillment and that of my brother. And yet I sense that I do not exist simply to take these guidelines seriously; I feel I'm on my way somewhere. To meet Someone.

Suddenly I see that beyond these moral guidelines those ancient people had indeed a towering point of reference out there in the wilderness. A great pillar of cloud with fire at the heart, reaching up to the heavens from the center of their camp. A cloud that moved! And they lived in relation to it. When the cloud moved, they moved. They sensed God somehow present in it. A God on the move in the world of men. A God calling them to follow Him. They could not tie their tower down to one fixed time and place, it could move at any time and in unexpected directions, and their life depended on moving with it. The God who led them also provided for them by giving Himself to them in word, in bread from heaven, and in water from the rock. Their life and identity depended on their relation to Him.

And slowly it dawns on me that my life also depends upon and grows out of this kind of moving relationship. Nothing static about it. And it involves personal giving and receiving, as I give myself to Someone Else and I receive that Someone Else as a gift. And slowly in Jesus I discover a man giving himself to God in a way that provided him with the inner freedom to do what God's love requires in threatening and confusing situations. So I begin to look to him for the humanizing of my life. He becomes my high tower. I sense God still on the move in this world of men, in Jesus. And all at once I find myself standing in the long shadow of the cross. Hammer in hand, nails in my pocket, here beneath the cross I stand. Suddenly life no longer seems so much a matter of self-realization as it does a matter of self-expenditure. I stand facing one of life's profound mysteries. And I begin to wonder, "What does this Christ require of me?"

2. FINDING A FOCUS

Life requires not only a point of reference but a sense of focus as well. I'm discovering a new understanding of faith in Christ that helps me with this. It's like putting on a pair of glasses after going for years without knowing you need them. You think you see quite distinctly. But when you have your eyes examined and glasses fitted, suddenly all sorts of things begin to clear up and come into focus. Depth perception improves. It's the same old world, but everything looks different.

One meets people who have gone on for years feeling they have most things under control. They manage to keep the misery and boredom down to a minimum and go along pretty well. It's just that now they have greater difficulty seeing where they're going.

I stood and listened to a man tell me about his experiences in the navy during World War II. Not that he relished the smell of death or the hellish waste of it all. Yet back then he felt worthwhile, part of a great cause. His life seemed to mean something, it was headed somewhere. But mercifully the war ended. Not so mercifully, in a real sense so did he. Like millions of others, he found himself discharged from the navy. But never since then has he really felt part of anything; he is rather like an outsider looking in. Now he feels that he works for little more than food and clothing. He has trouble seeing what's important. And when he tells me, "I feel like I'm going to pieces," I think he's speaking the literal truth. Anxiety gets him on the run now and then. Will he have enough money to get the children through college? What kind of job security does he have? Can he put something aside for the future? He's been taught to be anxious about a lot of things: money, security, sex, hostility, health, death. And he has learned how to worry about almost anything. Now he suffers from a vague sense of meaninglessness. And maybe it's because he has fewer meanings left unthreatened. He sees fewer things as clearly as he once thought he saw everything. His life needs a focus.

When I can't focus my eyes I get a headache. If I don't have perceptions in depth I begin to feel confused and insecure. Now some of my friends inside the church and some outside of it tell me that I shouldn't take Jesus too seriously. Yet I find in him a focusing of life that brings things into perspective. A profoundly practical man. He speaks to me out of his own experience. He talks like a man who knows how disappointment and bewilderment feel. He hoped to escape a cruel death, but didn't get his way. Still, he speaks of something he saw that helps me begin to get life back into focus.

Once Jesus said, "Where your treasure is, that's where

your heart will be . . . the eye is the lamp of the body, so if your eye is sound your whole body will be full of light, but if your eye is not sound your whole body will be full of darkness. If the light in you is darkness, how dark is that darkness!" And behind those words I hear Jesus saying to me, "Art, you need a change of outlook. Your sense of values is to your life what your eyes are to your body. If you can focus your eyes, then you can see things in perspective and avoid confusion." And he goes on to say, "Art, you can't focus one eye on one thing and one eye on another and make much sense out of anything. You can't serve God and Mammon. You have to choose."

Jesus doesn't tell me that I shouldn't serve two masters. He tells me I can't do it. He doesn't give me good advice, he states a fact. The Spirit of God and the dominant mood of human society lead in two different directions. They give me conflicting values. For instance, as Clarence Jordan suggests,[1] Mammon makes certain agreements with those who find the focus of their life in him. Mammon runs his show on the principle of profit. As long as a person is profitable, Mammon will take care of him. But if he gets sick or old, Mammon makes no promises. A man who derives his life-style from following Mammon had better make all the money he can while he's profitable; a time will come when Mammon will throw him aside. When that happens, this man will need all the resources he can lay his hands on to help him answer the question, "What am I going to eat now?" Jesus freely admitted that the followers of Mammon have to go after all the money they can get. Their system demands it.

Yet money gets mixed up in everything. The Apostle

Paul warns me against loving money. But I don't know who can escape it very easily. I can say that I don't love money—that I love my wife and family more than anything on earth. Yet my wife and I came fresh out of seminary with a new baby to a growing suburban church. For two years we lived on a subsistence salary which literally ate up our small savings account. If we had one or two people in for dinner, we actually went without food for the next week. But one of my wife's best girl friends had the good fortune to marry a young man with plenty of money and a flourishing business. Every now and then they'd invite us over for dinner. Believe me, I ate up! But then after a month or so we'd invite them to our house for dinner. Now, I didn't mind going without food for a week after such a soiree, but this friend really got to us when she used to say, "My, what fun it must be to live on a tight budget! How interesting and exciting it must make your shopping." She didn't know the half of it. And then she'd go on: "Having money is such a burden. So many people want something from you and you have to be so careful who you give to." Well, I didn't need to hear that kind of talk. I didn't find money a burden. I love my wife, I love my children, I want them to grow physically and culturally and mentally and spiritually. I want good housing for them and good food and good clothes and a good education. And before God I believe God wants at least this much for them too. But I can't get food or clothes or housing or education for nothing. I have to pay for them, and I often have to pay through the nose.

So love of my family gets all mixed up with love of money. The best and the worst in me mix and seem out of focus and confused. Yet the love of money in itself is all wrong because it can shut my eyes to the meaning of living. It can harden my heart and soften my head so that I begin to think of life in terms of money and not money in terms of life.

In our kind of world we all need money. And I don't hear Jesus saying that if I simply follow where God leads, he will solve all my money problems. Jesus remained poor all his life. He owned only one suit of clothes. He knew what working hard to earn your daily bread feels like. But when he begins to describe finding the focus of life in God he suddenly starts talking about the birds of the air and the lilies of the field. "See how God takes care of them!" And some of my friends say, "Sure, maybe God can take care of the birds of the air and the lilies of the field, but you better depend on your job and the health of the economy." Yet when Jesus starts talking about birds and flowers, I sense that he's trying to get things back into focus for me. He uses such words to get me to see beyond Mammon.

I begin to ask myself questions like "What does the value of money depend on? Where does it get its power to perform services? Does it have values in and of itself?" No! Money only has the value we give it. And that value rests on public confidence. The confidence of one man in another man, of one nation in another nation, of men in their government and of government in the people. An economy works only so long as this kind of confidence lasts. If a society fosters the antisocial feelings of people—if it caters to their fears, to their suspicions, to their hatreds—if it fosters reckless falsehood in high places and disregards the value of human life in a prolonged war—then you can hardly expect to come to the end of such an era and find public confidence and mutual understanding undamaged, and these are the spiritual realities underlying a sound economy. When an economy begins to falter, we suddenly face the fact that the spiritual basis on which it rests has been undermined. Strange how I missed seeing that for so long.

Jesus with his talk of birds and flowers helps me to refocus so that I can begin to think of money in terms of life rather than of life in terms of money. He says that I should "seek first God's kingdom." I've been created for that kind of environment. That means choosing life as my vocation. I've been created to live. I should begin to affirm my own existence. To love myself for my own sake as God does. Why does a bird or flower experience the care of God? Because they live in the environment for which they've been created. If a sparrow suddenly chose to live under water, would God take care of it? I doubt it. The bird would kill itself by choosing to live out of its environment.

For a long time I said, "No," to my own existence. I ran around trying to be someone else other people told me I was or should be. I played a lot of roles to hide myself, my loneliness, my weakness, my fears, and my resentment. But I paid a high emotional price for it in anxiety, depression and pounding headaches.

But suppose I don't have to prove anything to myself in order to love myself? Suppose I can love Art Sueltz not because he went to the University of California at Berkeley, took graduate study at Princeton Seminary, or because he's six feet tall and weighs one hundred and seventy pounds, or because he now serves the Presbyterian Church as one of her ministers, or because he's a good guy and gets along pretty well with people and makes those breath-taking contributions to committee meetings. Suppose I've been created to appreciate myself simply because I exist! Of course some things demand doing. Meals need cooking, songs need singing, old wrongs need righting. But some things need seeing and understanding. I need to see and feel that my sheer existence has meaning and importance to me and to God and to other men, over and beyond whatever I may do or how much money I may have. I've been built to live in that kind of environment.

And suddenly it dawns on me that when man first came from the hand of God, he came supplied with all the resources for the fulfillment of his life. He came into a friendly universe with plenty for him to eat and plenty for him to do. And that's been true ever since. Creation still has enough in it to meet the needs of all men living anywhere. The problem is not supply but distribution. The problem is not with God but with men.

And all at once so much I have missed seeing begins to come back into focus. Poverty and excessive wealth come when men choose to reject the values that will affirm their lives. In this light money looks sacramental—holy—as though it is somehow the body of Christ broken for us. In earlier days a man scratched out his little plot, planted his seed, and waited hopefully for the harvest so he could make his daily bread. God stood behind that whole process, so that seeds grew and men could eat. But today I don't grow my daily bread. It's only as far away as the closest supermarket. Yet I must have money to buy it. Money means bread to me. In fact, many of our young people use the two words to mean the same thing. Now, Christ spoke of the Communion bread as his body, broken for us. That had all kinds of meaning to a Judean peasant of his day. Suppose we substitute the words money or dollars for bread in the saying, "This is my body broken for you." Then every time money changes hands, we are somehow dealing with the body of Christ broken for us. Economics and business then become either Holy or Unholy Communion.

And as I begin to think of these things I sense the Lord saying, "Art, don't let your values get so out of focus that you miss the reason for your life. If you do you may put your trust in something that in the end will let you down. Seek first God's kingdom. Don't labor for the food that perishes, but for the food that endures to eternal life."

So my outlook begins to change. I begin to see more clearly things I had never seen or had long since forgotten. This new focus helps me to perceive how easily I could lose my life by trying to get the approval of people, or a certain financial security, all the while forgetting the environment that affirms my life. What kind of values will guide my behavior and shape my attitudes? That's something to worry about. Values—even facts—I once believed true have been challenged. What does it mean to follow Christ in a "greening" world?

3. THE GREENING BUG

As my sense of focus improves I begin to see a world bitten by the "greening" bug. I'm not sure when it all began. Somehow during the 1950s a great ideological struggle came to a head in the cold war between the United States and the USSR. We thought the nations of the world had to choose sides. But many emerging nations could not see enough difference between these two great powers to make a choice. Dr. James I. McCord of Princeton commented, "From their perspective, the two superpowers looked like two great giants locked in ideological struggle; but both are Western, both by Asians' standards are rich, and both are colonial powers." And so a third world emerged. However divisive the term may sound to some, it does take into account a new reality.

Furthermore, this greening bug bit an emerging generation in the Western countries. Not every decade brings into the public eye a younger generation so often completely out of temper with its parents. Values, even facts believed true by an older generation are challenged by a younger one. Something of this kind has always happened. But today many of our young people as they mature simply do not readopt older values. And this goes on not only in America but in France and Germany and Russia as well.

Peter Berger criticizes this "greening" of the world for its sublime disregard of the requirements of technological society and of the realities of power and class in America. He points out that the cadres of dissident youth have come overwhelmingly from the college-educated children of the upper middle class. And if they "drop out," he suggests, lower-middle-class children will take their place. This will give us the "blueing" of America. But he does give one warning. "There is one proviso—namely that the children of these classes (blue) remain relatively unbitten by the 'greening bug.' If they, too, should drop out, there would literally be no one left to mind the store."[1]

One day I picked up the Bible and thought I saw there a young man bitten by a distant ancestor of the "greening bug"—Absalom, the oldest son of King David. David stands out as a warm, vital, clearheaded, energetic man with the heart of a lion and the soul of a poet. Like Robin Hood, he whipped together a tough band of men and at the right moment seized power and led his country into a golden age. He ruled with an iron hand, but he had charisma and charm. Furthermore, he had a reputation for justice for friend and foe alike that fired people with a high sense of moral purpose. A sensitive and profoundly spiritual man.

But profound spiritual awareness is never a substitute for ethical integrity. The two are not exactly the same.

Piety and integrity do not always go together. On the one hand a man may have a high sense of ethical principle and no sense of any need for God. But if a person of great piety allows his feelings to run away with his behavior, his spiritual sensitivity may not save him from ruin.

And so I find David, in the prime of life, part of that group of adults who always carry the heaviest part of the world's responsibility. He has won his struggle to get ahead. His children have grown up. Young parents have so much to do that they hardly have time to indulge their neuroses; the father works long hours and the mother has her hands full with small children. The real crises come in the middle years. These prime years account for the highest number of cases of insomnia, alcoholism, marital difficulty, infidelity, neurosis, and psychosomatic illness.

Suddenly—unbelievably—in the heyday of life, David found himself involved with another man's wife: Bathsheba. In fact he plotted the murder of her husband in order to have her. David took Bathsheba into his home, and eventually she gave birth to Solomon. From that time on, David's house became a hotbed of jealousy and intrigue and petty rivalries—as though some things are forever wrong and their end forever tragic. His children matured in an atmosphere where they found trust difficult, and from these children the next king of Israel would come.

Absalom, David's strong eldest son, lived in that atmosphere. He felt it. He watched what went on. And what Absalom saw made him sick. He saw the hypocrisy of his father. How did this idealistic young man feel when the story began to leak out? It must have hurt. His warm, courageous father had done this! David, who had led his people out of economic depression—David, who worked and battled so that his children could live a better life—David, who fought some of his country's grisliest wars and turned back tyranny—David, his own father, who had done such great things, whom people loved for so many valid reasons—David had done this! That's what hurt.

Absalom watched his father temporize with justice. Maybe that's when the greening bug bit. How could he respect such hypocrisy? In the palace, one of his half-brothers raped Absalom's sister, Tamar. Why didn't the king do something? For years David had called down the wrath of God on all kinds of injustice. For years he had talked about ethics and morality. But now, with the chips down, he didn't do anything.

So Absalom dropped out of palace life and went to walk the streets of the city. There he listened to what people said, and let his hair grow long. He heard them complaining of lawlessness and how you couldn't get a fair trial from Dan to Beersheba. The whole system of law enforcement and judicial procedure didn't seem to produce justice any more. David had a reputation for being a man of the people, but he seemed to have lost touch. The government just didn't seem able to fathom the causes of trouble in the cities and the nation. Absalom wanted action. Action now. I suppose he might have waited a few years; he would be king when his father died. But to Absalom the problems seemed too great and too immediate. If ever a man belonged to the "now" generation, Absalom did.

For a long time I have heard preachers and others put Absalom down, as some sort of underhanded revolutionary. But when I stop to think about him myself I discover a young man with strong passions and high ideals. He doesn't look like just another plotter and schemer. Absalom won the respect of some of the leading lights in the intellectual community of the day: men of great integrity, including David's own chief counselor, Ahithophel.

And suddenly I see that Absalom was dead right and David dead wrong in much that happened. Things had to change in the country. Absalom could see it, David couldn't. Absalom ran out of patience. He just could not tolerate such grave, continued injustices any longer.

Now, whatever this may have to do with the "greening" of America or of the world, it sets me to thinking that God Himself must grow impatient with hypocrisy and injustice. And I begin to wonder whether perhaps the restlessness and disturbance in our world are not so much the results of our friend the greening bug as they are evidences of the impatience of God. The most disturbing factor in current affairs might well be God Himself. When a fresh, crisp, cold air mass sweeps down toward the Los Angeles basin and begins to hit moist, stagnant, smoggy air, it creates a storm front—turbulence, lightning, thunder, rain. But the storm often marks the coming of a change for the better in the weather. And I begin to wonder if the same may not be true of our time. Stormy times can mark the coming of changes long overdue in the affairs of men. David, beware! Don't live in the glory or the shame of your past. Be sensitive to the turbulent atmosphere of today's world. Today's world and today's generation need you. David, you sit in places of power and authority. Now is the time for you to act!

In this sense I am proud of the behavior of our own

Supreme Court in the last decade. That famous phrase "with all deliberate speed" grew out of the court's *Brown* v. *Board of Education* decision, commanding integration of the nation's public schools. But for fifteen years this meant to many people all deliberate resistance. Then, finally, the Supreme Court ran out of patience. In the first major judgment it made when the new Chief Justice Warren Burger joined the bench, the court unanimously ruled that the deliberate speed formula was no longer constitutionally permissible. In a brusque, unsigned order it declared: "The obligation of every school system is to terminate dual school systems at once and to operate now and hereafter only as unitary schools." As if to say, "David, the time has come for you to act."

Now if a period of rebellion has a great deal to say to David's generation, it also brings a word to Absalom's generation. If the times required action of David, perhaps they also required patience of Absalom. But Absalom could not wait. His impatience finally boiled over in a violent, bloody attempt at revolution. Sometimes in the Bible I think I can see God using revolutions as instruments of His judgment. But that does not mean that all revolutions and all revolutionaries are godly.

Absalom's revolution grew out of an impatience with injustice and a concern to change the structures of society that shape people's lives. But for all its sensitivity to issues and institutions it seemed to have little anchorage in concern for people and the relationships they share as persons. And there is little in Absalom's life to suggest keen awareness of any relationship to God. Lacking this profoundly spiritual dimension, for all his high idealism and moral integrity Absalom's revolution ended tragically for himself and his father.

The young man died, killed by his father's soldiers. But the whole turbulent era shook David to the roots of his conviction. At the end he stood with tears welling up in his eyes, "Absalom, Absalom, my son Absalom! Oh my son, if only I had died instead of you. My son, my son!" David sheds the tears of a man who knows that his unwillingness to do what simple justice demands has triggered the whole tragic chain of events.

Years later a crisp fresh breeze swept through Judea. Another and greater Son of David came out of Galilee. If ever a man demonstrated the impatience of God with the way things go, down on this earth, Jesus did. So fully human and yet so full of the life you'd expect of God. Wherever he went things happened. Often stormy things. Upsetting things. Things that heralded the coming of a fresh, new order. The Spirit of God got loose in Jesus of Nazareth and blew like a wind through the whole country. Those in authority couldn't see where it was all coming from, but they could see what was happening. Young people like Peter, James, and John and older people like Caiaphas and Herod for quite different reasons sensed in Jesus a quiet but radical revolutionary.

Writes Dr. James D. Smart,

> To the youth who think that devotion to a new age of justice and peace demands of them that they turn their back on the past, perhaps abandon faith in God who has been worshipped in the past . . . Jesus . . . may seem to be entirely too quiet, too patient with his opponents, and far too reluctant to seize the power that

would enable him to hasten the new age. They're impatient with quiet revolutionaries, they have no interest in the ministry of preaching and teaching, of liberating men as persons from demons, and opening up doors of life for them into the future. But they ought to listen and consider what issued from that quiet, undramatic mission of Jesus. Jesus was not interested in a revolt or a reformation that would run its course in one brief generation or less. His concern was for a permanent revolution. And in a few short years, in his life, his death, and his resurrection, he laid the foundations of that permanent revolution at such a deep level that ever since, each fresh encounter of men with him has become the decisive turning point between the world of the past and God's new age.[2]

Now that's not always an easy concept to get hold of. John the Baptist, for all his prophetic insight, remained uncertain about Jesus up to the end. Judas wanted action now, and remained so blind that he sent Jesus to his death. Saul of Tarsus, later called Paul, knew the Hebrew Scriptures backward and forward, but he first saw Jesus not as God's instrument of change but as the destroyer of all that centuries of faith had built up. Not until after Easter did Peter and some of those closest to Jesus begin to see in him the kind of changes God means to bring about. Jesus brought a unique spiritual dimension to the humanization of man. Here's someone who can save me from nostalgically romanticizing the past or excitedly romanticizing the newest idea. He takes me beyond the "greening" or the "blueing" of America to the discovery of an increased freedom to be an authentic human being, in love with God, people, and this world. Such inner freedom releases me to work for rapid, deep, and substantial change in the relationships of people and the institutions of our time. I think this is part of the essence of the Christian gospel: the necessity of permanent continuous conversion. All we do, all we build, stands to be corrected or replaced. Jesus reminds me of the relativity of everything to Him who is at the center of all.

4. ALWAYS IN TROUBLE

Always in trouble. T. R. Glover once commented, "Jesus promised three things to His followers. First, they would be entirely fearless; second, they would be absurdly happy; finally, they would always be in trouble." As I begin to sink down new convictional roots into the Christian faith, that last phrase of Glover's comes into sharp focus. Always in trouble. I grew up feeling that Jesus would get me out of trouble, not into it. Subtly, instead of putting myself at his service I had tried to use him for myself. I heard the preacher of a large church recently urging people on television to use Jesus as a means to achieve success in life. Another man said quite seriously that as he drives to the city he prays to Jesus for a parking place. And when he gets to work, sure enough, Jesus has provided him one. And then the other day I talked with a man who said that since he "gave his life to Jesus," his sales contracts have spiraled up. But suddenly I wonder if we know what we're saying in such remarks. That Jesus is simply our servant, out finding parking places for us, or clients——? Yes, Jesus helped people out of trouble. He healed the sick and raised the dead. But he also got himself into a lot of trouble. And I have to stop and reexamine what meaning that has for me.

Trouble comes to me in all kinds of shapes and sizes. Some of it is accidental. Some is unexpected. Some comes from my own stupidity. But nothing seems accidental, or unexpected, or stupid about the trouble Jesus got himself into. Many people loved Jesus, but many others hated him. I get a feel for the quality of his life from his enemies as well as his friends. Those who followed him began to see the issues of life focus with startling new clarity in him. Some tried to ignore Jesus. Pilate tried to wash his hands of him. But it didn't work for him, and it doesn't work for me. I can't ignore him. And I discover that when I begin to see the issues of life focused in Jesus I'm in trouble. For many important people in my life don't see things that way.

Some years ago I worked with Dr. James Forrester in a conference for college students. He told me of an experiment conducted at Stanford University. Researchers picked out six students who seemed to shape student opinion and create the emotional mood on campus. They invited these six students and twenty-four others to a room. On the board at the front of the room everyone saw three lines. Then they asked all the students to identify the longest line. But beforehand they had instructed the six student leaders to say that the shortest line looked the longest to them, all six said so. This had a profound effect on the other twenty-four students. In fact, only one of them had the inner strength and freedom to say that he thought the longest line actually looked longest.

Now, I have trouble saying what I believe is true if the important people in my life tell me that my eyes deceive me. Then I'm tempted to deny the truth of my own experience. In a way, I think Jesus anticipated this when he said, "Blessed are you when men revile you and persecute you and utter all kinds of evil against you falsely on my account." He knew the explosive nature of the movement begun and focused in him. Jesus made enemies as well as friends wherever he went. He knew that if I dared to follow him I'd be in the same kind of trouble. I, too, will be known by my enemies as well as my friends. Jesus made enemies when he moved against naked power and tactful half-truth in high places. Suddenly I see a storm building. The atmosphere feels charged with electricity as the fresh winds of God sweep through the stagnant affairs of men. And Jesus offers me no false hope. He never says that my eyes deceive me and there is no storm brewing. Nor does he tell me not to worry because he'll take care of everything. He's not that naïve, and I'm not that gullible. From somewhere deep inside I seem to hear him saying to me, "Art, this is it. You think you've been in trouble before. Well, you're just getting started! But I'm going to count on you. Don't let them scare you or make you back down. I think you're worth having on my side. Go to it. I'm with you."

Not that Jesus induces some kind of martyr complex. I've never sensed him saying to me. "Art, go out and look for trouble, because you won't know what real life is all about until you find it." That's neurotic and leads into the dead end of self-pity. A person trapped by self-pity will persecute himself if he can't find anybody else to do it. Nor does Jesus imply that all the trouble I get into is because I'm following him. People often criticize me, not for my goodness but for my lack of it. And they're often right. Often I'm not sympathetic toward the suffering of others, nor am I always sorry for my sins. Often I'm not eager to plunge into some fiery evil situation and do the hard work of reconciliation, even though I believe that only vigorous opposition to immense evils can redeem history. I see that issue focused in Christ as nowhere else. As the winds of God blew and the storm broke there flashed across the darkness of this turbulent, discouraged world a life of unwavering integrity, compassion wide as the sea, love that won out over evil, and purity steady as a rock.

No wonder that, when it comes to the dark clouds of injustice, or racism, or poverty, or war, Albert Camus—himself not a Christian—said, "What the world expects of Christians is that Christians should speak out loud and clear and that they should voice their condemnation in such a way that never a doubt, not the slightest doubt, could rise in the heart of the simplest man, and that they get away from abstractions and confront the blood-stained face history has taken on today."[1]

Now, I'm a minister in the church of Jesus Christ. And I suppose any preacher can be popular if he's halfway eloquent and affirms the prejudices of his listeners and urges them to use Jesus in the achieving of their already established goals. But I find myself getting into trouble when what I see in Jesus does not conform to such goals and ambitions. Who likes to listen to somebody who goes around poking holes in your favorite ideas or pointing out stupidity or evil in your highly valued opinions? Like many people I tend to defend the prejudices I learned as a child, even when deep within me I know a prophet is speaking the truth. And my society has subtle ways of dealing with men who dare to stand for human dignity in the face of vested interest. Let a senator speak out for peace and international cooperation and what happens? Immediately criticism swirls around him. "What's he trying to do? Does he think he can change human nature?" As Dr. John A. Mackay once commented, "He will face the resolve of the sons of mammon to maintain by force those forms of social order that are responsible for the dereliction of the poor."[2]

So if anyone begins to move like Jesus to disturb unfettered self-interest, he may get called all kinds of names. People called Jesus a winebibber and a friend of sinners, a blasphemer, and in league with the devil. If they could have made such labels stick, they might have discredited him and destroyed his effectiveness. Today I find the names have changed, but the technique remains much the same. Like little boys calling names over the backyard fence, people call sincere followers of Jesus "radical" instead of friends of sinners, or "Communist" instead of blasphemers, in the hope of horrifying respectable people and reducing the Christians' effectiveness. Some organized groups make a profit out of this kind of thing. And however you may conceive of the devil, I've come to respect him as a past master in the use of the red herring.

And so I am discovering the kind of trouble I'm in for when I take Jesus seriously as the point of reference for my life. I may not die on a cross or burn at the stake, but I can get burned in many other ways. If I stand for racial justice and open housing I may become suddenly very unpopular in my own suburb. Today in Rhodesia, the church of Jesus

Christ provides the only organized force standing in the way of rabid racism based on the pattern of South Africa. "There are moments in the life of a church in a country," comments one of Rhodesia's church councils, "when giving witness requires one to say with John the Baptist, 'It is not lawful, O king,' there are moments when the well-being of his flock requires that a pastor humbly defy Caesar in the name of the Lord." And Caesar will react! In neighboring South Africa, *Time* magazine reported, ministers have lost their passports and been detained and charged with subversion of the country. And I have to ask myself if I'm willing to get into that kind of trouble for Christ's sake.

Yet I remember the sense of shame that has come over me when through fear I tried to avoid getting into that kind of trouble. The times when fear sealed my lips, when I knew I should have spoken out against obvious evil. My own sense of self-worth seems to call for a willingness to endure such provocation. Furthermore, in those times when I throw my fears to the winds and state as clearly as I can as much of the truth of Christ as I know pertaining to a given issue, I find that even my vulnerability sometimes wins the grudging respect of those hostile to me. After all, who respects a man who agrees with everything and never stands for anything until he sees which way the wind will blow? And I get to wondering how that handful of people who first followed Jesus made such an impression on the world? Did great preaching do it? I doubt it. They didn't have very many great preachers. It looks as if ordinary people simply got into trouble because of what they saw focused in Jesus, and won the grudging respect of a hostile society.

And so I begin to understand a little why I will always be in trouble if I take Jesus seriously. I will go to the trouble of standing up for the powerless, the poor, and the exploited today because Jesus did in his day. So often such people have no advocate in the councils where decisions are made that affect their lives. But if Jesus is there, someone must speak in his name. Doing so may mean challenging the established authorities. Often in the heat of such encounters people can discover the presence of the Lord.

There's an old story about a king who built a great image, symbolizing all that his government stood for. He wanted the whole nation to bow down to the values symbolized by this huge figure of himself. Trumpets sounded, and everybody bowed down except three men. Dragged before the king and threatened with death, they continued to refuse to acknowledge any authority higher than the God of Abraham, Issaac, and Jacob. So the king decided to burn them alive and had the furnace heated up. They were in real trouble. But as they faced the fire, Shadrach, Meshach, and Abednego said, "If so be our God whom we serve is able to deliver us from the fiery furnace, he will deliver us out of your hand, O King. But if not, then be it known to you, O King, we will not serve your god nor worship the golden image you have set up." So off they went into the fire.

Then suddenly a tense hush settles over the whole scene. The king himself goes to the entrance of the furnace to see what's going on.

"Didn't we throw three bound men into the fire?" he asks.

"Yes sir."

"Then why do I see four men loose, unharmed, and walking in the flames, and one of them looks like the Son of God?" It's the presence of the fourth that makes all the difference when men get into trouble.

5. OF PRINCIPLES AND PREJUDICE

Sometimes I mistake my prejudices for principles. It happens sometimes when I try to apply my understanding of Christ to the issues and events of my time. And nothing blinds me to the truth so much as a prejudice parading around as a principle. Political prejudice blinds me to valid criticisms and perpetuates old evils. Class prejudice can tear an economy apart and put blue- and white-collar workers into two warring camps. Racial prejudice can separate me from my brother before I even know him. And religious prejudice can get my eyes off God and allow me to make judgments without really looking for the truth. I remember when a fiery Protestant minister, Ian Paisley, went all over Northern Ireland making derogatory statements about the evils of Roman Catholic Christians, thoroughly confusing his prejudices with his convictions. But I noticed that when Irish Protestants and Irish Catholics began to shoot at each other Ian Paisley conveniently ducked beneath his pulpit, and has since moderated his stand.

Yet I also have inherited the prejudices as well as the principles of my people. And often, with words like "school busing," my prejudices surface under the guise of principles just long enough to let me know they're still there. I even hear some political leaders inviting people to oppose the law of the land and the whole concept of law on the basis of their prejudices.

Now Jesus once ran into a man who seemed to have confused his prejudices with his principles. A lawyer. At that time the laws of God and the laws of the land went together to make up one body of law. To make practical sense out of any of it a lawyer had to be an expert in theology as well as jurisprudence. This man qualified as an expert in both. He sat one day listening to Jesus trying to help people sort out their values. Finally this man asked, "Teacher, what must I do to inherit eternal life?"—a question meant to test the competence of this amateur from Nazareth. Hardly batting an eye, Jesus answered, "Why, a man like you knows all about the law. You tell us. What does the law say we should do?" Taking the bait the man summed everything up in the two great commandments: "You must love the Lord your God with all your heart, and all your mind, and all your soul, and all your strength, and you must love your neighbor as yourself."

"You're right," responded Jesus. "Do this and you will live." And he sounded like a teacher giving a pat on the head to a slow learner who had by some miracle come up with the right answer. The lawyer felt foolish and deflated. Trying to salvage something, he continued, "But teacher, who is my neighbor? Where should I draw the line?" Instead of giving him a direct answer Jesus told a story. Dr.

George Buttrick used to speak of the stories of Jesus as "earthly stories with heavenly meanings." I think he had a point. But as I've begun to read these stories over again in recent years they have a way of getting beneath my skin. All too often they disturb my prejudices by bringing home to me resented, distasteful, and sometimes difficult truth. If that's what Dr. Buttrick meant by "heavenly" then OK. But the cutting edge of truth I now feel in the stories of Jesus takes me beyond what I had thought of as heavenly. These stories hurt. They have a way of laying my heart open before God. Maybe Jesus learned how to tell stories like that by reading the Old Testament prophets.

Dr. James Smart in his book *The Quiet Revolution* makes one see how the Old Testament prophets used stories to open a man up so that God's word had a chance to get heard.[1] The prophet Nathan once stood before King David, who had seen Bathsheba and wanted to make love to her. Unfortunately she already had a husband, but David could take care of that. He had sent the army up north to settle a border dispute; someone had to die for the country—why not Bathsheba's husband? So off to the front Uriah went, and died in the heat of battle. Using his authority quite legally, David simply murdered the man. He didn't see it that way at the time, but he certainly didn't fool the prophet Nathan, who had a sharp eye when it came to principles and justice.

Now Nathan stands before the king to relate a story. He tells of a poor man who owned one little lamb. The whole family loved the little lamb and made a pet of it. Then suddenly, without warning, a wealthy neighbor seized the lamb and made a banquet of it for a guest instead of using an animal from his own great flock. This unjust, unprincipled, act outraged David. He swore that such a man should die. But hardly had the sentence crossed his lips when he saw the prophet's upraised finger pointing at him: "Thou art the man."

Now that kind of story hurts. Nathan didn't simply have some vague spiritual truth he wanted to illustrate. He went straight for the heart of the king. A story like that in the hand of a prophet gets under a man's skin. Nathan didn't want to teach David some new ideas about God; he wanted him to see something that might save his soul! That's the point of the story. Not ideas, but life. Not indoctrination, but revelation and redemption. The kind of insight that may lead me to change the direction and style of my life. Such stories lean heavily on my tendency to condemn quickly in others the very faults I'm blind to in myself. My conscience works beautifully when the situation doesn't involve me. But that same conscience has strange blind spots when turned on myself.

The story of Jonah involves many of the same dynamics. A prophetic writer faced a confused mixture of principle and prejudice in the mood of his country. A growing narrow nationalism, a zealous "love it or leave it" mood seemed to pervade everything. People saw other countries chiefly as objects of God's judgment. The old idea upon which their nation had been founded, that it existed to be a blessing to all the countries of the world, didn't interest them any longer. So under the guise of telling a story this prophetic author tried to lay bare the soul of the nation. And he had a sharp sense of humor.

Sometimes playful ridicule can prove more powerful

than the strongest argument. The currently popular television program "All in the Family" is a case in point. A recent edition of the "Southland Sunday" supplement of the *Los Angeles Times* carried the following letter: "When we caught the opening show of 'All in the Family,' I remember an announcement apologizing for the dialogue even before the program started. Can you tell me exactly what it said?"

The editor answered, saying, " 'The program you are about to see,' the voice cautioned, 'is "All in the Family." It seeks to throw a humorous spotlight on our frailties and prejudices and concerns. By making them a source of laughter we hope to show in a mature fashion, just how absurd they are.' "

The author of the book of Jonah wrote in much the same vein. How people must have smiled when they heard of God asking Jonah to go to Nineveh and preach—why, that's like asking a member of the John Birch Society to go on a Quaker peace mission to Hanoi or Moscow! Like Jonah, he'd probably take a ship in the opposite direction as fast as he could. Jonah didn't want any part of God's plan to save the Assyrians from their well-deserved destruction. And yet he did a selfless thing when he let himself get thrown overboard by foreign sailors who he believed would lose their lives because of his disobedience. In a given situation the most prejudiced man may not lack compassion.

Now Jesus told this kind of story to a man who had confused his prejudices with his principles. The story has a surface meaning—we should be kind to anybody in trouble. But Jesus hid a sharper point beneath the surface, one designed to help a man distinguish between prejudice and principle. He used this story to lay open his heart. An offensive story, that tale of the Good Samaritan—to a Jew of the time there were no good Samaritans, only bad ones. Jews and Samaritans hated each other. So Jesus didn't preach merely in the abstract about loving our enemies. He brought everything right down to earth. Maybe the nearest I can come to the shock value of the story today would be to translate it something like this: After a famous American industrialist and a noted American preacher had passed by, a Chinese Communist came to where the beaten man lay, and when he saw him he had compassion. In that setting I seem to hear Jesus saying to me, "Art, here's a man who, according to your views, has all the wrong ideas about God and society. To you he's not only your enemy but also an enemy of God. But as he goes down the road he does what God wants done. Now you have a choice to make. Who stands with God? The man who has all the right ideas about God but little compassion for the victim by the roadside, or this hated unbeliever who cannot pass by a man in bitter need?"

What a story! Jesus pointed out that God might find true believers beyond the limits of orthodox Jewish religion and culture, but he hid that distasteful truth beneath the surface of the story. Going around telling stories like that, it's sometimes a wonder to me that they let him live as long as he did. When he had finished the tale he asked the lawyer to give his verdict upon who was a neighbor. The man gave the only answer he could, and in giving it he passed judgment on himself—whether he knew it or not, who can say? So Jesus disregarded the surface questions about fine points of theology and went right to the heart of what disturbed the integrity of this man's life. He put his finger on that sore point, and it hurt.

Late one night our youngest son, Gary, woke up with a pain in his stomach. The clock said three o'clock, so we told him to take an aspirin and an antacid and try to go back to sleep. But the pain persisted and moved down into his lower abdomen. The doctor stopped by on his way to church, pressed down on the abdomen, quickly released it, and asked, "Does it hurt?"

Yes, it hurt! So Gary went into the hospital and at seven o'clock Monday morning had his appendix out. In much the same way, Jesus brings pressure to bear on the sore points in my life. And then he takes out this kind of a story and uses it like a scalpel, without much concern as to whether or not it hurts the patient, for he's out to correct a condition that may endanger my life! Jesus wants to get beyond my prejudices so I can sink the roots of my conviction down into the truth and love of God. He's not trying to make a fool of me, but he will apply the kind of pressure that may open me to the fresh work of God's grace in my life.

And I get the feeling that he works this way not only with individual people, but also with churches. I mean, I grew up with certain prejudices about the kinds of things churches should properly do. I had some pretty strong religious prejudices. And Jesus continually brings pressure to bear on these sore points. Once in a while I hear someone saying, "Why doesn't the church stick to it's own business?" And behind those words I hear the religious prejudice that churches ought to stick to making believers in

Jesus and training them in their devotional life. As if to say, "Make me a Christian, but don't tell me how to use my money or my political influence to relieve oppression or human need. The church shouldn't get involved in those things. It should stick to preaching the 'gospel' and ministering to the soul, but everything else—war, poverty, race, birth control, housing, matters of government—should be left to the layman's conscience." And that sounds reasonable until I think back over a little recent history. Then I remember that this idea of the church's business is exactly the one that totalitarian powers still hold! After World War II Martin Niemoller, whom Hitler banished to a concentration camp, told of an interview he once had with him. Hitler stormed against the church's interference in political and social matters. "You can deal with heaven," said Hitler, "but the German people on earth belong to me and to the state!" And today many Communist countries have pretty much the same point of view. Churches in Russia can worship more or less as they please, but there are severe restrictions against any social activity. And a church pronouncement criticizing any official state policy is just out of the question.

Now I can hardly blame Christians in Germany for going along with the Nazis if they were conditioned to think that the church should be entirely unconcerned with affairs of the body politic. But in Germany there were Christians who could see beyond that prejudice, and they formed an anti-Nazi confessional church. This church did not have political action as it's primary objective. Of course not. They preached Christ above all. But these Christians saw the implications of some of the Nazi policies and had the courage to get together and condemn them openly in the Barman Confession. And who today would want to say that a church that condemned anti-Semitism in Nazi Germany was not minding it's business, and "should have kept quiet"?

Of course I really believe that churches have a primary responsibility to preach the gospel and offer worship to God. But I also believe that preaching the gospel is not something that concerns only my religious interests. Jesus came in the flesh and cared about every aspect of my life. He cared about my religious principles and my religious prejudices. And he told a story that seems to say that if our business as Christian churches is to bring men and women to God, it is surely also our business to try to feed them if they're starving. And if we have a responsibility to care for their bodies as well as their souls, surely this responsibility extends to the body politic, where decisions get made that affect human welfare. So I sense Jesus bringing pressure to bear on the sore points in our corporate lives as Christians to try to get us to examine our confused mixture of principles and prejudices in the light of God's love and truth.

I hear him calling me to stand for that truth, and as I hear that call I sense the shadow of the cross falling over me. Stand for God's truth in this world? A man could get killed standing there!

6. ATTITUDES AND ASSUMPTIONS

I often have as much trouble with my attitudes and assumptions as I do with my prejudices and principles. I arrived on this planet unprepared for life. I had no previous training or practice sessions. So very early the attitudes and assumptions of people around me began to shape my own attitudes and assumptions about other people and other ways of life. But now as Christ assumes a more central position in my life I find that many of these attitudes and assumptions have no visible means of support. Some years ago a Cincinnati rabbi told a Jewish boy that he could no longer go to the Presbyterian Church gymnasium and swimming pool. So the boy went to the young Presbyterian minister whom he liked so much and tried to explain. But the young fellow could only stammer, "Ain't religion hell?" What I see depends on my assumptions. It isn't so much that seeing is believing. Believing is seeing.

Dr. A. A. Robach once gathered a choice crop of international insults into a dictionary of slurs. (Someone asked him why he hadn't also included a section on international compliments. "There aren't any," he replied.) His collection contains many old and new slurs, all directed at "dirty foreigners." For instance, the French call syphilis "the Spanish disease," but Spaniards call it "the Italian disease," while the Italians call it "the French disease." How shocking to think that Jesus would ever have stooped to a racial slur! One day a Gentile woman asked him for help and he insulted her. "It isn't right," he said, "to take the children's food and throw it to the dogs." There it is, right in the New Testament. And if I can't face it squarely I'm hardly ready to take his gospel seriously. Few incidents in his life raise more questions than this one about his attitudes and assumptions. The words have a hard racist sound. They just don't sound like Jesus. So for years Christians have tried in one way or another to make out that he didn't mean them as they sound. But suppose Jesus not only said these words, but meant them! What then did he mean?

He had taken a short trip outside Judea into Gentile country. Why he went we don't know. Some suggest that it was to escape the long arm of Herod's police. He'd been getting in deeper and deeper all the time, and the possibility of arrest grew with each day; Herod's police had no jurisdiction in the district of Tyre and Sidon. Still, we don't in fact know why he went there. We do know that his disciples went with him. And we know that when this Gentile mother came up to Jesus asking for help, Matthew heard it all and remembered to write it down so that none of us would ever forget. "Son of David, Sir! Have mercy on me! My daughter has a demon and is in terrible condition."

At first Jesus didn't say a word. Not a word. No response,

just silence. The kind of silence that makes me wonder what's going on inside the head of this strange Galilean. Was he confused as to how he should respond? I doubt it. Jesus knew that the Old Testament prophets treated racial prejudice as being as great a denial of God Almighty as atheism. So I get the feeling that he hesitated on purpose. He created a strategic silence to allow the attitudes and assumptions of his disciples to come out into the open. A Gentile woman stood asking a Jewish man for help, and Jesus must have known what was going on in the minds of his disciples. He had grown up breathing the same air of Jewish superiority they had breathed, and he knew what a corrosive effect that can have on the human spirit. How then could he help them deal with such ungodly attitudes and assumptions? First he had to make them see that they had them! So he remained silent. He created a space quiet enough for those basic assumptions and attitudes to surface.

Sometimes I need a period of silence in the presence of Jesus because I myself have trouble coming to terms with the basic assumptions of my life. There's nothing quite like a little silence in the presence of Jesus to get these things out in the open. Take for instance the whole matter of racial prejudice. As Welch Alden suggests I too during the past ten years have spoken and worked for fair housing and for open housing and for equal rights and for equal opportunity.[1] I've served on committees and I've tried to preach the truth of God as he has given me to understand it. And I've taken my share of criticism for it. So that when I sit down next to a black man and hear him lumping me in with a lot of people whom he labels racist, the hair on the back of my neck begins to stand up. I don't like being lumped in with those people, and it doesn't seem fair.[1] But then one day, sitting in the silence before Jesus, I find myself having to admit that I did grow up in a part of society where almost all institutions reinforced a basic assumption: that it's better to be white than black. I have to admit that I grew up breathing that air.

It's been so easy to fool myself into thinking it isn't true. Sure I work with blacks, I cheer the desegregation rulings of the courts, I weep at the death of Martin Luther King; but in the silence, when I look into the eyes of Jesus, I seem to hear him saying to me, "Art, you think you're free of attitudes of racial superiority? Well, tell me, would you like to have been born black in America? Would you willingly trade places with any black person today? Art, we've both heard some people say that blacks get all the breaks—fast promotions, preferential treatment by the government—but tell me honestly, would you like to trade places with any of them?"

And in the silence with Jesus some of my basic assumptions and attitudes begin to surface. Like his disciples, I have absorbed them almost by osmosis. Their attitudes came out into the open in their response to the woman and her noisy demands. The disciples, not Jesus, spoke first. "Send her away! She's following us and making all this noise." She annoyed them. And plenty of times I've felt annoyed by the noisy demands of blacks or chicanos or some other group. I mean, sometimes I've just walked over and turned off the TV rather than listen to another tirade against some injustice to this or that group. Maybe that's the way the disciples felt.

"Lord, send them away! Tell them to find their own solution. These are their problems; I've got enough problems of my own."

But in the New Testament story the woman kept on with her vociferous demands. One of the February 1972 issues of *Life* magazine carried pictures of the famous bus boycott sixteen years earlier in the South, and of Martin Luther King in prison. Yes, we've made some progress since then, but I wonder if we'd have made it if it hadn't been for the noisy demands of people about the conditions under which they lived. I doubt it. Many of us in the fifties were pretty well satisfied with the way things were going. But these loud demands helped force our attitudes and assumptions out into the open.

Jesus finally broke his silence to echo the attitudes of his disciples, as if to say to her, "You heard them. I've been sent to the lost sheep of the house of Israel." But then he went on to add, "It isn't right to take the children's food and throw it to the dogs."

And I think his voice had an edge to it. Words can cut two ways. Jesus often spoke like that. Many a time the story he told cut in two directions simultaneously. At dinner once in the home of a Pharisee he told the tale of a loan company which forgave two men their loans. A secular story with no mention of God in it, and yet it brought judgment on the Pharisee who heard it, while assuring forgiveness to the woman who sat drying his feet with her hair. Jesus' story of the Prodigal Son had the same effect. Jesus often made his words do double duty when the situation called for it.

Now suddenly he senses a Gentile woman ready to put

her faith in him, while at the same time he feels the assumptions of his disciples about her coming through in their words to him. Jesus could feel it because he, too, had lived as a faithful member of the Jewish community. A faithful member and yet a critical one, a nonconformist member. And it's not easy to remain faithful and nonconformist at the same time. It's not easy for me to be faithful to my heritage and yet be critical of it.

David Woodward tells of a friend of his, a bank president —a man who believed in equality and justice very deeply but never spoke publicly about these deep convictions. So Woodward asked him about it. The banker looked him coldly in the eye and said, "Now back off, Dave, remember I'm a banker and I can't afford to offend people."[2] And that reminds me how difficult it is for me to even try to be in, but not entirely *of*, the middle class into which I was born. Yet it's not impossible. Not impossible to be in the world but not of it. If it were impossible, then the whole life of Jesus Christ would be a lie! For Jesus simply did not unquestioningly embrace the assumptions and attitudes of the people he grew up among. Even as a boy of twelve in the Temple he raised questions about the things people seemed most sure of. In his day, as in mine, they had certain assumptions which they simply accepted without much thought. All through his life Jesus seemed to move right in on those centers of agreement and shake up people's security. He seemed more interested in the truth of God than in what they had agreed upon. So he would wade right in and raise the right questions in all the embarrassing places. He didn't drop out. He remained loyal to his culture by standing within it and challenging all its unexamined attitudes. He wanted to force them out into the open to defend themselves.

For instance, those around him assumed that Jews were born with more ability, more brains, more character than any other people. Jesus did all he could to undercut that assumption. In this instance his disciples wanted him to get rid of this woman. She bothered them. They probably wouldn't have acted quite that way if she'd been Jewish, but she wasn't. So Jesus played along with them long enough for their real notions and prejudices to surface. But he played a deadly serious game with them. While expressing and exposing their attitudes, at the same time he wanted the woman to know that he didn't want her to leave. A man can say something with his lips and something quite different with his eyes. At any rate, this woman didn't give up when she heard his words. She could tell the difference, somehow, between his rhetoric and his meaning.

Martin Luther, commenting on this passage, once said, "The woman heard Yes when Jesus said No." These two seemed to understand each other. Jesus said, "It's not right to take the children's food and throw it to the dogs." And he meant the words to sound hard and cutting, for he had to expose the full heartlessness of the assumptions and attitudes he had grown up amongst. But they didn't crush this woman. Far from it. When she heard them she seemed as happy as a martyr when the fire won't burn. She seized on the hardest word of all—"dogs"—and played along with him. "Yes, Lord, I'll gladly be your dog, if you'll let some of the crumbs from your table fall on me"—and that ended the game.

Christ's word cut one way exposing the attitudes and assumptions of his disciples and another way exposing the great faith of this woman. He didn't have to berate his disciples; suddenly they knew what he'd been doing. They stood exposed. Then Jesus brought it all to a close saying, "Oh, you're a woman of great faith." In one stroke he complimented her faith and rebuked their narrowness. These men had simply taken the gospel of Jesus and added it to their own habitual reactions, and as a result their Christian faith became so fused and confused with their inherited attitudes and assumptions that they stood in danger of hopelessly compromising and concealing it.

So I hear Jesus speaking to me about some of my own inherited ways and notions—for I have them! And I can't just wrap them up like an unwanted baby and leave them on some other doorstep. I've got them, and they're all mine. And I find myself wondering whether or not I really expect to make some new discoveries about what it means to follow Christ in this world at this time. Do I look forward to any revolutionary changes in some of the basic attitudes and assumptions I've learned to live with? Can I grow beyond them, and if so how? And I think Jesus shows me how. He did something. He acted to meet this woman in her need. Her daughter was healed instantly. As if to show me that I can grow beyond my narrow, restrictive ways and ideas as I concentrate on meeting the needs of people. Extending myself to meet a man's need takes me beyond his racial origin or political point of view. When I look to Jesus I see a man at his most appealing and inspiring as he moves through the narrows of the assumptions and attitudes he inherited, out into the great depths of human need, and I try to follow in his wake. I'm coming to believe more strongly than ever that Christ in his life, death, and resurrection offers me the hope that God can really change my own attitudes and assumptions, and in the process change me so that I can overcome evil with good. Thank God for such a Christ! He seemed to know that I could not go on the way I am.

7. SHOULD I DO EVERYTHING I'M ABLE TO DO?

As I begin to move out of the shallow waters of earlier attitudes and preconceptions, other questions arise in my mind. Should I do everything I'm able to do? What about sex? Not a new question, but for those just entering their thirties and forties a real one.

A minister in his mid-thirties picks up his phone and hears a feminine voice on the other end asking if she can come in to see him on an urgent personal matter. He agrees to see her in his study. At the appointed time there she sits in a stylish basic black dress. He recognizes her as a member of his congregation. A young woman, just barely thirty, full of life and vitality. She begins to tell him that since she's no longer married she's having a terrible time coping with her own strong sexual urges. "What am I going to do? I can't go on unsatisfied like this." And then she invites the minister to come home to bed with her. Out of the ordinary? Perhaps?

And what about young married women out in the

suburbs who after they've gotten the kids off to school, form car pools and head for town and a little sex with agreeable young men during the long "executive" lunch hour? Or what about the young wife who goes to work as a secretary in a large city office and has to cope with three propositions in one day? Or what about the young nurse who finds carrying on three affairs simultaneously very attractive except when one or the other of her lovers begins to get possessive? And she finds it a little tricky fitting the care of her five-year-old-son into her schedule.

Or what about the distinguished professional man, with a strict religious background and strong sexual impulses, whose wife could care less about sex? At worst she refuses to participate and at best simply lies there like a lump. He can't bring himself to have an affair with another woman and finds himself humiliated and guilt-ridden reduced to masturbation.

So now what happens to that strong attraction between man and woman—call it sex or love or lust or just procreation——? Whatever I call it, it still represents a tremendous power that can make me happy as an angel or as miserable as the devil. And somehow in the crucible of this powerful reality my potentialities for integrity and consideration and sacrifice as well as for selfishness and greed and evil come to the surface. Ought I to do everything I'm able to do?

Like many people I talk to, I too have trouble coping with this tremendous sexual power within me. Particularly now on the threshold of middle life. More infidelity to marriage partners seems to happen in this period than at any other time. Most divorces also seem to occur in middle age. And I've noticed that most nervous breakdowns, most serious emotional upsets, also seem to take place then. Sometimes a man says to me, "Religion is good for my kids. I drop them off for Sunday school. And it's comforting for older people." As though any man worth his salt should be able to make it without such a crutch. But the truth seems to be that a lot of us in the middle years need a little help. Some tell me, "Art, you'll find the help you need" in a new product or by developing a new system of government or business or some new theory of psychology. As though I could come up with schemes so clever that I would not have to be good.

Now, I don't find Christ putting down attempts to deal with the external events and needs of life. He knows that I need food—he fed the hungry. He knows I need health—he healed the sick. Yet he never seemed to allow his concern for these externals to take the place of his concern for my inner self. Time and time again he moves from the laws that govern behavior right into my inner feelings. As though he knew that in the inner citadel of my soul I have to cope with the power of my own sexuality. In that inner secret place I must ask myself, "Art, should you do everything you're able to do?"

In the 1920's people began to break out of the straightjacket of Victorianism. But now a lot of us are struggling with how to express our sexuality in a way that will humanize and fulfill us. And we've had some suggestions along the way. Some say, "Trust your feelings. Whatever makes you feel good is right, and whatever makes you feel bad is wrong." Yet if I took his suggestion seriously I could condition myself to feel good after sex with no thought of any continuing human relationship.

So in troubled times some of us would turn to sex just

out of sheer boredom. The most advanced civilization in history, with the highest standard of living ever known has somehow produced a lot of bored apathetic people. Men get out of bed in the morning with nothing ahead that makes the day look very interesting. They go off to work wondering if it's really worth the trouble. Worse yet they have few pleasures in which they have much fun. How often when a person says, "I'm tired," he really means, "I'm tired of doing what I'm doing. I'm tired of living the way I'm living." Some seem to hope to find in sex the stimulus that their mental or emotional or physical environmental fails to give them. But can I satisfy my hunger for life by simply concentrating on a fragment of it?

Furthermore, blatant sex may not be so much a search for identity as a symptom of its loss. Suppose that the current wave of pornography grows out of a new sense of sexual insecurity rather than a new sense of sexual freedom. If so, I doubt if it will do much good to pass stricter antipornography laws—much of the deluge of pornography that has washed over us suggests that people have reached one of those times of spiritual depression when they go to bed because they have little hope and nothing better to do.

So, both in the "counterculture" and in "straight society" many seem ready to throw off the chains of restraint. Here are a young man and woman who sincerely believe and deeply feel that they have a special relationship. Something so special that it exempts them from the grubby, outworn restraints of sexual behavior. Right now they both feel that having sex together fulfills and humanizes them. Then after a few months they begin to find tensions in their relationship for which their earlier assumptions had not prepared them. What happens now may cripple them for future relationships. People seem prone to injure themselves by an act of self-giving they cannot sustain and to which they were never deeply personally committed.

So now we've got beyond the repressive Victorian restraints, but where shall we look for the developing of a happy, fulfilling, intelligent sexuality? Katherine Anne Porter describes the dilemma of many in the counterculture in a revealing passage of her book, *Ship of Fools.* A girl reflects on her relationship with a young man: "They had agreed in the beginning not to marry because they must be free, marriage was a bond cramping and humiliating to civilized beings: yet what was this tie between them but marriage, and marriage of the worst sort, with all the restraints and jealousies and burdens, but with none of its dignity, none of its worth and protection, with no honest acknowledgement of faith and intention."[1]

Now I've begun to rediscover that when God created sex He created a good thing. But I'm also beginning to see that the idea that I can treat my sexual partner as an attractive but disposable item is as old as hell. That idea dehumanizes a person by treating him or her as a thing. And I can't relate to things and persons in the same way. I'm beginning to see that to simply treat sex like an appetite such as hunger or thirst doesn't take my total sexuality seriously. I simply can't take a woman to satisfy a sexual desire as I would take a drink of water to quench my thirst. As Benjamin Garrison suggests such a temporary "relationship" with a woman isn't really a relationship at all. "It lacks meaning, dignity, depth, and climax!"[2]

When I turn to Jesus to get my bearings I sense that he takes my sexuality seriously. Of course I don't have a direct line to Jesus, nor do I hear voices. But I do sense something going on within me that corresponds to what Jesus began to do and say in Galilee and I attribute that to the continued working of his Spirit. And so I ask at the point of my sexuality, "Lord, should I do everything I'm able to do?" And what I hear from Jesus does not sound puritanical or narrow. He seems rather to get under my skin and reach right down into my feelings. It feels like someone trying to save me from a disintegration of my person. Someone who knows the dehumanizing distortions my sexuality can suffer. I hear him reminding me that authentic sexuality can get confused with eroticism, that is, enjoyment without relationship. If I do not appreciate the wonder of my own sexuality I can easily distort the importance or value of another person. That can happen in marriage as well as out of it. People do not exist to be used but to be loved—loved by being with them as they are. Not as I need a person as an object for my use. I've known people to get married on the basis of sexual enjoyment. What they really said to each other was, "I love me and want you." A very possessive kind of arrangement. And I've known others who get married on a kind of fifty-fifty basis. They say to each other, "I'll love you as long as you love me, but not any more than you love me and not any longer." That's a little more congenial, but not too much more life-affirming. In Jesus I begin to see a better way.

To love a person as he or she is I believe means giving rather than receiving. A personal commitment without guarantee. A commitment I'm willing to sacrifice for. And that kind of relationship means giving the most precious thing I have: my life. Not necessarily that I'll die for someone, but that I'll give her what's alive in me. I'll share with her as openly as I can my thoughts, my joys, my interests, my understanding, my humor, my sorrow, all that's going on in me. In giving my life I find I create an opportunity for her to come to life. Not that I'm trying to get something back, but as life wells up in another person I can't help receiving. My willingness to give helps make her a giver also. And then suddenly we both share in the joy of what we have brought to life together. In the act of that kind of unconditional giving something is born and both of us are involved. And I hear Jesus saying that God meant for such giving to be so complete and so permanent that neither person is ever the same again. "For this reason, a man shall leave his father and his mother and be joined to his wife, and the two shall become one."

And as a man I am beginning to discover that this whole relationship has aspects to it that I had not thought of. Here's a young woman at the end of a day as taxi driver to the Little League, the Blue Birds and the Y as she rushes to get dinner on while she's trying to fix in her mind her committee report to the PTA, discovering that she has less and less energy to be someone in her own right. And she feels it deeply. Everywhere they go she's always introduced as her husband's wife. Later that evening, lying beside her husband, she begins to feel that she exists only for and through her children and her husband. And then she begins to wonder why marriage and motherhood should be a total way of life for women when marriage and fatherhood has never been a total way of life for men.

Today both men and women face new decisions about each other. Once perhaps society seemed to define woman's role, rather clearly, but it's not so clear any more. And in the confusion I look for Jesus. I sense him still moving among the people of the world promoting the equality of women with men, treating women primarily as human persons and willing to contravene social customs to do it. The New Testament gives no hint that he ever treated women as inferior to men. That's extraordinary when I think back to the culture he grew up in.

When Jesus attended Synagogue the rabbies didn't allow women to even read the Scriptures. One first-century rabbi, Eliezer, put it like this: "Rather should the words of the Torah be burned than entrusted to a woman. Whoever teaches his daughter the Torah is like one who teaches her lasciviousness." Furthermore a woman couldn't testify in court. Her testimony didn't count.

But Jesus never seemed to have time for such repressive customs. When he began to preach he talked to all kinds of women personally and in public. And from what I can see he talked with them as human persons, not as "sex objects." Furthermore he time and time again explained the Scriptures to them.

And Jesus deliberately rejected the Jewish idea that a woman's testimony didn't count. Easter morning Jesus appeared first to a woman! Jesus made a woman the first person to bare witness to the central affirmation of the Christian faith. Through her testimony men first heard what had happened.

All the way through his life I see Jesus trying to get across the fact of the equal dignity of women. Once someone challenged him on his understanding of the nature of God. In response Jesus told three stories in a row. Each of the stories reveal an aspect of his understanding of the nature of God. His first story had to do with a shepherd who left 99 sheep to go out looking for the one lost. "God is like that" Jesus seems to say. The third story tells of a Father welcoming home his prodigal son and having some straight talk with that son's older self-righteous brother. "God is also like that" Jesus seems to say. But in the second story Jesus talks about a woman who turned the house upside down looking for a lost coin. And Jesus used a woman to reveal God's nature! "God is also like that." Who but Jesus would have thought of that at that time in that culture?

I see Jesus strongly promoted the dignity and equality of women in the middle of a male-dominated society. Can I do any less? Through it all I seem to hear Christ saying to me, "Art, give yourself in ways that will free women, your wife, your daughter, your friends, to be the persons they are meant to be. That may require some changes in your attitudes and behavior. But don't take women or their place in this world for granted just as I have never taken you for granted." And I have to decide whether or not I will dare to alter my thinking and my behavior in ways that will affirm in my wife and all women a new sense of self-worth and personal dignity.

8. AMBITIOUS FOR WHAT?

Ambitious. That's how I started out in life. But ambitious for what? Living soon began to feel like a continuous tournament. Very early I got the feeling that if I took the right courses, met the right people, memorized the right procedures, smelled good, and smiled, I'd succeed. I simply grew up in a success oriented community. That fact I believe affected my relation with men and women and God. In our community let a boy hit a home run in Little League and someone starts talking about big league material. Even schoolteachers told me that every year spent in school meant more dollars in my pocket. As I grew older the beat went on, although now I discovered that a man's friends, his bosses, and his family all have a bearing on his success. Their success or failure affects his standing in the community.

This striving for status can not only bring on personal confusion but corporate confusion as well. Here's an aggressive young executive who feels his company must have a computer. Why? Because everybody knows that any successful, aggressive enterprise has a computer. The fact that he knows relatively little about computers or their value to his operation gets pushed to the back of his mind. He simply feels that his operation needs the status that goes with having a computer. And what happens? Suddenly months later he finds himself damning the computer for bleeding his operation white. Simply having the computer did not insure good lines of communication within the operation. It had instead contributed to corporate confusion rather than corporate productivity. All of which again raises the question, ambitious for what? Confusion at this point can even affect the way some men in business answer their phone. The phone rings. How will it affect his status if he picks it up without first letting his secretary relay the call?

And I also discovered this ambition to succeed blurring the focus of my faith in Christ. I've seen preachers and churches trying to show that God is really at work in them by pointing to the number of members on the roll and the size of the budget. As though God always honors faith with that kind of quantitative success. Yet an awful lot of people seem to feel that He does. Not long ago I heard of a sincere man who said, "Last year I only made thirty thousand dollars, but this year I really obeyed the Lord and made my first half-million." And I begin to wonder, why then did Jesus end up without a penny and on a cross?

Like a lot of other people I'll probably never get my picture in the newspaper, or write a best seller, or turn the world upside down, but I am trying to get Jesus back into focus in my life. Somehow his poverty and the great struggles and frustrations of millions of his best people make me feel that the way some preachers measure success may have nothing at all to do with real religion. Ambition does play an important role in my life, and—I think—in the lives and efforts of most people. It gets people moving. But ambition for what? That's the question. Ambition in itself seems ethically neutral. It can motivate the "Godfather" or Pope John. And I find myself having to ask in what sense I want to succeed? The answer I come up with will play an important part in the shaping of what I say when I preach.

As I get Jesus more clearly into focus I see again that a man cannot serve two masters. Do I really want to serve God or am I simply ambitious to build a big church? A friend of mine, minister of a large, affluent suburban congregation, recently confessed that he didn't dare preach on the Sermon on the Mount. When asked why, he said honestly, "It would blow my congregation apart." A man's ambition affects what he will dare to say. Some time ago the *New Yorker* carried the cartoon of an urbane-looking older minister who stood talking to a young chap. "Drawing on my not inconsiderable experience, Andrews, my advice to a young man ambitious for preference in our calling is to steer clear of two subjects—politics and religion."

Yet William James once remarked that religion is always a dull habit or an acute fever. And God seems to prefer crude life to antiseptic death. Someone said of Prince Albert, the husband of Queen Victoria, that he passed himself around in small cold pieces. And some people give themselves to me like that. Often cold slices of tongue. But other people pass themselves out in great warm chunks, and I usually come around for a second helping. They're energetic, ambitious people. And this sort of person seemed to appeal to Jesus; at least he chose some for his closest friends. James and John, so full of energy and ambition that Jesus called them "Sons of Thunder"—two tough, aggressive fishermen in whom fierce competitive tempests could break out as quickly as a storm over the Sea of Galilee. Once these two ran into a faith healer who seemed to heal people in the name of Jesus. But neither James nor John had ever seen him around Jesus. So they confronted him and asked, "Do you belong to the disciples of Jesus?" The startled healer admitted he didn't, and James and John told him to quit healing. These powerful, ambitious men liked devastatingly simple answers to complex issues. They belonged to the "in" group around Jesus and didn't want any outside competition. Later they told Jesus, "Master we saw this man who wasn't one of us healing in your name, so we made him quit."

John Redhead points out how this spirit survives today. Two ministers worked along side of each other in some community effort. When they finished the project, one said to the other, "After all, our differences are much less important than our agreement. We're both working for the same great end."

"Yes," replied the other man, "we're both doing the Lord's work, you in your way—and I in His!"[1]

Jesus had no time for such an attitude or assumption. "No one who does a mighty work in my name will soon afterward be able to speak evil of me. He that isn't against me is for me." And I discover that in spite of my ambition to be part of the Lord's "in" group he continues to surprise me by the unlikely people through whom he chooses to work.

Toward the end James and John traveled with Jesus to Jerusalem. For some reason Jesus had decided to go through a city of Samaria. Usually Jews avoided it if at all possible. So much bad blood ran between these two peoples that Jews took long detours around the place. But this time Jesus took a short cut right through the heart of Samaria. He couldn't telephone ahead for reservations for the evening, so he sent a runner. The man came back with word that the city wouldn't allow Jews to stay overnight. When I read that I thought about a town where I once lived which had a law just like that about black people. But I also remember a time when I took my wife and family to a well-known restaurant for dinner. We'd saved our money and all looked forward to it. My children had on brand-clean school clothes. But the manager looked us over and didn't like the clothes my children had on, and though he had space, refused to serve us dinner. He made me blazing mad. I think I know how James and John may have felt. "Lord, let's call down fire and burn up the whole place. That'll show them!" Kill for the love of Jesus. But Jesus wouldn't hold still for that. Hate for hate just wasn't part of his nature.

Finally, on their way to the Last Supper these two competitive, ambitious men got to arguing with the others about who should have the top administrative jobs when Jesus finally made his move and took over. Then James and John got Jesus aside and asked for a little preferential treatment. "Lord, let one of us sit on your right hand and the other on your left hand when you come into the kingdom." They wanted to be Vice President and Secretary of State in the new administration. And I get the feeling that in spite of three years with Jesus the ambitions of James and John ran something like this: I'll get all I can for myself today and I'll take my chances on getting even more tomorrow. This didn't necessarily make them mean or greedy; it just made them resemble most people. They could treat people they liked with warmth and generosity, but they wouldn't give one little bit of themselves for somebody who didn't matter to them. James and John were simply the most important people in the world to James and John. They even tried to "get ahead" among the men who followed Jesus.

And I find myself getting caught in that same trap. I mean, I attend church meetings and serve on committees and teach classes and call on people and pray and tithe. Then one day I saw how much of it was simply my ambition to "get ahead" of some other preachers. All for the glory of God, of course! And as I look around among other Christians I sense the same tendency. Yet Jesus seems to go on choosing those ambitious competitive people and making some of them his closest, most trusted friends. He seems to look for people who have no time to take their time.

Right there at the end it looked as if he'd failed with James and John. Ambitiously they asked for the top jobs in the kingdom. "You don't know what you're asking for," said Jesus. He just won't allow men to be grasping and stay happy, selfishly ambitious and at peace. Ambition isn't bad. The direction it takes is critical. Jesus was an ambitious man. But Jesus Christ, "though he was in the form of God did not count equality with God a thing to be grasped, but emptied himself, taking the form of a servant being born in the likeness of man." I suppose Jesus might have been ambitious to rule the world as Caesar and Alexander tried to do. And I think he could have done what they attempted. But his ambition got him going in a different direction. Instead of trying to be preeminent and lord it over men he made himself their servant. And that raised the issue of how the world will be saved. Will the world be saved by ambitious men anxious to get ahead, or by men ambitious to serve the needs of other men?

Yes, I'm ambitious. But for what? And again I seem to hear Jesus saying, "Art, remember me. I could have chosen to rule the world like another Ceasar. All for the glory of God, of course! I deliberately chose instead to serve you and every other man. I chose not to stand on my dignity, not to demand my property rights, not to demand my family rights. I chose instead to put myself completely at God's disposal, as his servant in meeting your needs. That meant absolute dependence on Him and total loyalty to Him. Art, you too have some choices to make."

And as I try to think through what he means I remember how at that Last Supper he took off his coat and got down on his knees before James and John to wash their feet. One final effort to get the explosive power which was locked up in the ambition of these two men moving in a new and creative direction. James and John wanted to get ahead and fill themselves with honors, and suddenly they saw Jesus on his knees in front of them. It didn't look natural to see so strong a man humble himself like that, and do it so unpatronizingly. It seems far more natural to demand service. It's very hard for me to stop assuming that I deserve a few little extras. James and John, ambitious for preferment, wanted to be served rather than serve. Even after three years with Jesus and all those long talks about love and sacrifice, when it came right down to it all James and John could think about was what they could get from Jesus for themselves. And I realize how long I walked with Jesus and related to him in much the same way.

Then I hear some jarring words, "Art, you see how men of the world like to 'get ahead' and exercise power over people. That's not the way I want you to live. If you want to get into the stream of real life you must follow me as God's servant of men. Even the Son of Man did not come to be served, he came to serve and give life to redeem many people."

Now when I sense Jesus talking to me like that I feel very threatened. I feel threatened because I think of my ambitions as my own private property. They're personal, they belong to me. They're my business. Jesus turns all that upside down. He speaks as though I don't use my ambitions as tools in life; he speaks as though my ambitions use me as their tools. Ambitions have to find people they can use. That's how they survive. They need representatives. They need me. And I have to make choices. I have to choose what purposes will use me. How tragic, if some old ambition which has thrown its weight around in the world for centuries, breaking hearts and causing sorrow for millions, finds a fresh instrument in me! Selfish self-interest is not as private and personal as I had thought. It's a world-wide ambition that knocks at the door of almost every man's heart. And when it comes along Jesus says, "Friend, that ambition knocking at the door of your heart is an old one. Look as far back as you like and you'll find homes wrecked, friendships shattered, wars fought, all because of the drive to get ahead of the other guy if at all possible."

The closer I look, the more it seems that Jesus talks to ambitious people something like that. It's as if he were forever trying to get us to allow him to fill us with a new purpose: that of moving out into the stream of life as he did. As God's servant to men. "As the Father sent me, so send I you." And I think that kind of a reorientation requires an act of God within me. I'm not at all sure I'm strong enough or secure enough in myself to pull it off. Who but God can work such a radical change of nature? But then, suppose God *is* at work within us. "Few of us ever experience pure unselfishness. But whenever we get close to it, we know that the good we do seems to be done through us rather than by us, even though we choose to do it. It's like swimmers supported by a strong tide; I swim, yet not I but the tide is with me."[2] So God will help a purposeful man move out into the life-affirming current. A man gets his direction from his God. And whenever we're talking values we're talking God, whatever words we may use. What a man values most he serves as his God. That makes it terribly important which God I choose. If I choose the God and Father of our Lord Jesus Christ, then his ambition becomes mine. "For God so loved the world that he gave——!"

Theodore Roosevelt once read a book by Jacob Riis, called *How the Other Half Lives.* It told about the terrible conditions of the day in New York City and made such an impression on Mr. Roosevelt that he made a special trip to call on the author. But Riis wasn't at home, so Roosevelt left his card with this note on it: "Dear Mr. Riis, I've read your book and I've come to help." And God's book has begun to impress me in new ways. Sometimes I feel like saying, "Oh God, I've read your book and I've noticed again your desire to build brotherhood in this world and to establish peace among men, to proclaim the release of the captives, the recovering of sight to the blind, and to set at liberty those who are oppressed and proclaim the acceptable year of the Lord—and Father, I've come to help."

9. I HAVEN'T LIVED YET

In his novel *Doctor Zhivago* Boris Pasternak describes a young man facing execution. Guards drag him along with several others to the edge of a cliff for shooting. Suddenly this young man breaks out of line, falls to the ground, and begins pleading, "Forgive me, Comrades, I didn't mean it, it won't happen again, but don't kill me, I haven't lived yet." How haunting that last phrase: "I haven't lived yet"! Suppose I should die before I live?

At seven o'clock one evening a man looks up from his desk. How he envies a man who works from nine to five on a day like this! He slams a desk drawer shut with one hand and picks up his coat with the other and without bothering to button his collar or straighten his tie heads out of the office. He's had a good day—worked hard but done a good job. Hard to guess his age, somewhere in his thirties or forties. Just as hard to guess his income, somewhere between fifteen and thirty thousand. He's achieved many of the goals he set out to achieve. Now he protects those achievements with insurance policies and securities and retirement benefits. He's got life pretty much under control. As part of the establishment he makes the city run. Besides that he serves on the Boy Scout board and gives time to other volunteer agencies. He has everything.

Yet driving home tonight he begins to wonder. Sometimes he feels he hasn't started to live yet. What does all his work add up to anyway? He's begun to hear criticism of the Protestant work ethic. But is it a sin to work hard? Is it a sign of rotting conformity to strive for excellence? Doesn't a man act responsibly when he puts his abilities and talents to use? What would happen if everybody dropped out and refused to make any contribution? Yet he often feels like little more than a mirror reflecting what he thinks other people expect of him. A kind of dull reflection at that.

This Sunday he'll take his family to church. But he frequently feels he's had enough religion to last a lifetime. Maybe it's his age. Maybe it's the crawling pace of the freeway traffic. As he sits behind the wheel he begins to feel a little depressed and slightly confused. In fact this feeling has been coming over him off and on for the past few months. So he turns on the radio for a little relief, or at least distraction. Searching for his favorite station, he hits one of those all-day, all-night religious broadcasting outfits. A man comes on with a heavy preachery twang and grinds out some miserable old clichés about Jesus. He can't turn the thing off fast enough. The voice, the whole approach irritates him. But Jesus—well, he's read about a new wave of "Jesus People." Yet they don't seem able to tell him what he longs to hear either. He doesn't question their sincerity or enthusiasm or human warmth, but many of their ideas of God seem out of touch with the realities he lives with every day.

For a minute he tries to get beyond other men's ideas of Jesus to examine his own awareness of him. He knows that Jesus never had the kind of bank account he has, nor did he have a steady income, nor did he sit on any decision-making boards. Yet he seems so full of life in the area where this man now feels so empty—so strong where he himself feels so weak. Life *must* have other dimensions, or even his own achievements will begin to lose power to hold his interest. Life is beginning to be dull. He's beginning to feel he simply hasn't lived yet.

Around sixty generations ago a man in similar circumstances felt he hadn't lived yet and thought he recognized in Jesus what he'd been looking for. I think that's what drew people to Jesus. Not so much his preaching, not so much his miracles, as Jesus himself. For once on our earth people thought they saw a man on fire with life, and they came out to see him burn. One day this young man pushed through the crowd and fell to his knees in front of everybody and pleaded, "Good teacher, what must I do to have life like that?"

"Don't call me good," answered Jesus. "Save that for God." The words hit him like a blow between the eyes. They got his attention but hardly gave him the information he'd expected. Have you ever wished you could open the New Testament and find a direct answer of Jesus to a specific question? I have personal problems and specific questions about lots of other issues. But Jesus, in the gospel and in my own experience, seldom if ever comes straight out and tells a man what to do. The really great men don't offer solutions. They keep pointing to reality and asking, "All right, what about it?" Jesus kept pointing to God and to the world. "Don't call me good. Look at God. Where do you stand with God? When you figure that out, decide what you ought to do about it."

The way this man said "Good teacher" told Jesus something about his attitude toward God, religion, and life. A hard-working, decent man, he wanted information about what he could do to relieve the boredom and dullness of life. He'd grown up feeling that if he did all the right things he'd find fulfillment. Why then did he feel so empty? Why wasn't his best good enough? After all, sometimes you get tired of doing the right thing. When he said "Good teacher," he implied that Jesus was a good man like himself only more so. He wanted Jesus to tell him what extra thing he could add that would fill him as full of life as Jesus was.

But there stands Jesus saying, "Don't call me good. Look at God. What does He tell you to do? Do not kill, do not commit adultery, do not steal, don't bear false witness, don't defraud, honor your mother and father." The man looks up in confusion. "Teacher, I've done all that since I was a boy. What are you talking about? I've done the 'right thing' all my born days, and it still hasn't brought me life." And that's exactly the point! This man didn't lack respect for the commands of God. He had tried to live by them for years. What more could he do? He hadn't lived yet and he knew it.

Jesus looking at the man didn't envy him, didn't resent his prosperity—he loved him. He seemed to want him for a disciple. "You lack just one thing." How Jesus could simplify! He had a way of going for the jugular vein. "Just one thing. Go sell everything you have and give it to the poor and you'll have treasure in heaven. Then come and follow me." Incisively Jesus cuts through much confusion in my sense of values. Here's the issue: I may have the right ideas about God and an orthodox understanding of God's word and at the same time be psychologically uninvolved with God. I can believe in the God who made me and at the same time be psychologically controlled by the gods I make. That's the issue. Who and what is really God to me? This man in front of Jesus needed to know, as I need to know, that God claims precedence over all other loyalties, relationships, and interests. Along with many others I often feel as if any total claim of God on my time or priorities or my political philosophy or my material goals threatens my existence. So I find myself getting defensive. And one of the very best defenses against that kind of radical claim is a decent life built on trying to do the right things and substituting that for the control of God in my life. As though I could have God as some sort of extra ingredient to add flavor and zest.

But suddenly I notice that Jesus didn't tell this man to try harder to do the right thing. Try harder! The man had already done that and it hadn't worked. Nor will it. "Try harder" isn't the gospel. It's hardly good news to tell a man who's already doing all he can to try harder. Advice to try harder didn't draw people to Jesus. Is that all he had to say to the woman who washed his feet with tears and dried them with her hair? How could I believe in him if, when she looked up through her tears, he had simply said, "Try harder." What kind of hope does that offer desperate people? If Christianity simply means trying harder to be better and dredging up what inner strength we can to do it, then —let's face it—God cannot give me life, and it's up to me to find it on my own. And then suppose one tries to do that for years and still finds life less than he knows it could be.

I don't hear the word sin used much, or in many churches, anymore. So some of us go on suffering from an ailment without a name. Still, we use the word in other contexts and it sounds exciting. A theater marquee suggests all the exciting things that happen to the star because of "her sin." Fascinating stuff. But Jesus saw sin as the life-destroying element loose in the world: a lack of faith in God that results in the taking of life completely into our own hands. I choose something else and allow it to assume the role of God in my life. Anything else. "Go, sell all that you have and give it to the poor." Immediately I get defensive. Impractical. Overidealistic. Suppose everybody did that. "Great idea, Jesus, but it won't work in my life or in my world." Then suddenly I see that, though I may believe in God, when it comes to the crunch I also have other loyalties that come first, and God second. A man has to ask himself, if it comes to a choice between his job and his God, his political point of view and his God, his house and his God, his place in the system and his God—how will he decide? He may, like the man in the story, find himself terribly torn up inside but choosing his job and his house and his place in the system every time.

So again I seem to hear Jesus saying to me, "Art, I can't ease you into the new life you're looking for. Pain accompanies every birth. Look at the men and women who first took a chance on me. They didn't find it painless and easy, nor will you. You may have to get rid of some opinions you've hung on to for years, opinions that make you feel secure and superior. But if you really want life you'll have to take the risk of trusting God and giving up whatever you've been using for a security blanket. That may mean your prejudices, or a favorite habit, or the esteem of a few important people, but whatever it is, get rid of it."

And I hear myself answering, "Wait a minute, Lord. I'll tithe my income, I'll support the church with my interest, I'll work for justice and peace and equal opportunity in the world, but there are limits. Now you've gone too far. You've asked too much." But again I sense the shadow of the cross falling over me. I hear Jesus calling me to stand with him there, giving myself to God and men sacrificially to free men from selfishness and sickness and poverty and racism and war and sin. And I hear him saying, "Art, if you think living for God in this world is a tame little tea party, try it!" And standing there in the shadow of the cross I think I begin to understand how the rich young man felt when he turned his back and ducked for cover.

I know Jesus didn't ask everybody to give away all their money. Yet I can hardly read this story without feeling that Jesus thought money and possessions almost invariably prove a serious obstacle to putting oneself unconditionally at God's disposal. Jesus seems to make unreasonable demands. By reasonable I mean what we usually expect. But then, Jesus did not speak or act in ways we usually expect. He asks me to leave behind the irresponsibility of doing nothing more with my life than my own thing and building my own private world.

"When the man heard this, gloom spread over his face and he went away sad because he had great possessions."

He wanted the kind of life he saw in Jesus, but not that much. He simply could not give up his world in order to share in God's. Jesus asked him to get involved in meeting the needs of the poor. After all, hadn't this man sensed God giving Himself away in the life of Jesus? God making His resources for living available to deserving and undeserving people without distinction—— But faced with a decision as to whether he would use his resources sacrificially to affirm life as God does, this man decided he'd rather use his resources primarily to protect himself. Jesus wanted him for a disciple. He might have been another Peter or John or Paul. But as someone suggests, he remains any anonymous property owner worried about taxes and inflation, who grabbed for the world and lost it. He might have influenced history except for his business interests and his bank account in Jericho. These things hadn't satisfied him before and they would not satisfy him now. He hadn't lived yet. He would go on in the future to speak sadly of his property rights and property values and to call for repressive measures against restless disadvantaged groups and miss God and the life offered in the gospel.

He "turned sadly away," says Mark. And Jesus let him go! Sometimes in our statistic-minded church structure I lose sight of that. Jesus lost some outstanding people. So far as I can discover he failed ever to convert this man. Jesus refused to snare the hesitant against their will. He longs to hear me say Yes, but he will not interfere with my No. Unfortunately, as a minister I sometimes try to be more tactful than Jesus. I can't remember ever coming right out and asking a man for a big chunk of his income for the work of God. But Jesus did. Usually I try to get a man interested in the church first and expose him to some of its needs and hope he'll take the hint. As Halford Luccock used to say, we modern Christians would have taken the rich young ruler and made him chairman of the finance committee and said to ourselves, "He'll grow—he'll grow." And sometimes a man can get on the inside of the church and feel Christianity is something that it's not. Some feel that Christianity should be nothing more than a warm, life-affirming way of life that offers everything and makes no hard demands. Christ minus a cross. But Jesus never offered that kind of easy religion. He never hid the cross at the heart of our faith. He just went on in his transparently honest way pointing to God and asking men to let go of their lesser loyalties and choose life in Him.

At least one young man turned sadly away. And I've learned again these past few months that no one turns his back on the kind of costly commitment Jesus asked for and walks away happily. I've watched people in our church weigh the cost of a life-changing, mind-changing commitment to Christ and turn and leave for a more agreeable religion. But none of them went happily. Some left in bitterness and some in tears and some with a sigh of dejection. The New Testament checks with my own experience on this point: no one turns his back on Jesus Christ and walks happily away. I wonder if they sense that they haven't lived yet.

10. BUT GOD——

Dr. E. Stanley Jones says, "The early Christians did not say in dismay, 'Look at what the world has come to,' but in delight, 'Look who has come to the world.' " And I catch that mood everywhere in the New Testament in little words, words like *if* and *and* and *but*. Especially the little word *but*. "They laid him in a grave, but God raised him from the dead." Later Herod threatened to stamp out an infant Christian church, "but the word of God grew and multiplied." That little word *but* reminds me that things do not always turn out the way I expect.

A year ago my father visited South Dakota, where my grandfather had homesteaded. Looking at a field of corn he said to his brother who still farmed the place that it looked like a fine stand.

"Yes," said his brother, "but if we don't have some rain soon, we'll have no crop." My father returned home and after a few weeks phoned his brother and asked about the corn.

"Well," said his brother, "we did have four inches of rain, but we may lose the crop if it freezes."

And I suppose we all use this little word *but* like that. Someone says, "Of course I believe in God, but——" Thus, as I once heard Dr. Louis Evans say, "we go sliding along on our buts!"

Now it seems to me that the early Christians took that little word and turned it around. They tell me that King Herod threatened to finish off the church. He threw the leaders, Peter and John in prison and cut off James's head. The membership began to disperse, "but," they add, "the word of God grew and multiplied." Later I hear Paul saying, "we are handicapped on all sides, but we are never frustrated. We are puzzled, but never in despair. We are persecuted, but we never have to stand it alone. We may be knocked down, but we are never knocked out."

Yet life sometimes stands up and takes me by the throat. It just refuses to live up to my highest hopes. So many brave starts end in disillusionment. And disappointments and disillusionments begin to do evil things in my mind. I disappoint myself. I had hoped I'd be someone far stronger, far more human, far more consistent than I am. Sometimes I feel like nothing more than a patchwork job of leftover parts and pieces. I get to feeling like one man who said, "I'm supposed to be a father, and a husband, and a salesman, and an employee, and a church member, and a homeowner, and a member of the Veterans' Club, and a Little League committeeman, and an American, and an all-around-good-guy. And I try to play all these roles. But I get pulled first one way and then the other and I end up confused. Then I get angry and fed up with it all."

Not only do I disappoint myself; my religion sometimes disappoints me. I think that's the greatest disappointment of all, to feel disappointed in God. "He trusted in God," they shouted under the cross, "that God would deliver him. If God thinks so highly of him, then let God deliver him now." And it looked as if God had gone on vacation. Nothing happened. Time dragged on and Jesus died. I wonder if he knew how my human disappointment in God feels? This strong young Galilean set out from Nazareth to win the world for God. Suddenly, life stood up and took that dream of his by the throat. People would not have his gospel. His crowds dwindled. His best friends denied him and ran. His enemies hung him out to die. It looked like the end of everything. "My God, my God, why have you forsaken me?" Jesus died.

"They laid him in a grave, but God raised him. . . ."

If that's true, it feels as if someone has opened a window for me on a whole new world of reality. It sounds like news from another network. Someone telling me that you can't stop springtime when it starts to come. Jesus first appeared like God's springtime breaking through the winter of man's discontent. A warm, full-of-life-and-laughter kind of man; a man who enjoyed parties. When he walked into a room, everybody cheered up. He brought life to the party.

But life didn't treat Jesus very kindly. It threw discouragement and disappointment in his face and finally killed him. Death did something terrible to Jesus—"but God. . . ." Nobody knows how God did it. Yet Mary Magdalene weeping outside the tomb suddenly dried her eyes, and frightened men in an upper room burst out into the street stammering good news. You can't stop springtime when it starts to come. Jesus lives!

The events and the later reports confused many people.

Two such persons just had to get away from it all. They couldn't sleep. In fact the whole past week seemed unreal. Every time they closed their eyes they could see the three men hanging there in the hot sun with the flies swarming around. They still had knots in their stomachs and couldn't eat. Nor could they stop their ears to the sound of the hammer echoing across the valley. Nothing seemed to fit any more, nothing seemed right. Once they had been so sure. Now they felt insecure. Everything looked confused, out of joint. They just had to get away, so the two of them set out for Emmaus.

Where is Emmaus? Well, someone has suggested that Emmaus is wherever you go, or whatever you do, just to get away. It can be a trip to the movies just to see the show. It can be drinking a cup of coffee that you really don't want. Emmaus means whatever you do or wherever you go just to get away.

But how could they get away from something like that? Everything they once held so important seemed to die with Jesus. Now all their values and assumptions seemed up for grabs. They hardly noticed the stranger who joined them. Neither could remember seeing him before. He walked along quietly, listening to them trying to sort things out. Finally he asked, "What is it you are talking about?"

So they stopped in the middle of the road to answer. "Are you the only man in Jerusalem who doesn't know what happened there these last few days?"

"And what was that?"

"Haven't you heard what happened to Jesus of Nazareth? We used to hope he had what it takes to straighten things out and get this country moving again.

We thought we saw in him the promise of a new day. We still feel he was the one. Indeed, we heard God speaking to us in him as we never heard God speak before. But our leaders wanted no part of him. He was crucified. In his last moments on the cross we heard him say, 'It is finished.' Now we've begun to wonder if God has finally had enough of us. It looks like He finally got fed up and just decided to let this world go to hell." Thus they may have spoken of their broken dreams and shattered hopes.

Daniel Moynihan, speaking some time ago at Notre Dame, commented, "What is it that government cannot provide? Well, it cannot provide values to persons who have none or who have lost those they had. It cannot provide meaning to life. It cannot provide inner peace. It can provide outlets for moral energies, but it cannot create those energies. In particular, government cannot cope with the crisis in values which is sweeping the Western world."

But suppose this strange traveler still walks the highways of our world. Suppose I too can hear him saying, as those earlier two men heard him, "Don't you see that the Christ of God couldn't help suffering like that in this kind of world? Don't you understand the Scriptures?" What man takes kindly to someone threatening his special privileges or poking holes in his personal prejudices? Jesus made trouble for himself when he upset the tables in the Temple. He made trouble for himself when he put down the institutionalized formality of religion and stressed instead acts of justice and mercy and faith and love. When Jesus made religion painfully relevant to everyday issues he angered conservative religious people who think religion should not meddle in these affairs. Jesus told stories to make people think and ask questions and get into arguments with each other and with him. But most people want to hear easy answers and vague spiritual generalities. For centuries—since time immemorial—demagogues have capitalized on man's hunger for easy answers to life's hard questions. Jesus refused to do that. Most men have longed for a hero who would give them a straight Yes or No, so they could avoid the painful process of having to reevaluate their lives. If God's Christ keeps making them think and reevaluate their basic assumptions, they will begin shouting "Away with him!"

Starting with Moses and the prophets this stranger on the road to Emmaus began to explain from Scripture why among our kind of people God's kind of Christ necessarily suffers. The two men on their way to get away from it all suddenly felt the rationale for what had looked so irrational beginning to burn inside of them. Like fire it lit up their whole inner landscape. The sun hung low on the horizon, casting long shadows. The little town of Emmaus grew quiet as people went in for dinner. A dog barked off in the distance. With a little urging, their strange new friend accepted their invitation to dinner. Nothing fancy about the meal: a few loaves of bread and something to wash it down with. Their guest picked up the bread and gave thanks for it and broke it. And I don't know what it was —maybe as his sleeves fell away from his hands, and they saw the scars—but suddenly they knew! It was the Lord!

And then, "He was gone." I'm grateful to Dr. Theodore Parker Ferris for insight into the significance of those three words.[1] Those three little words now make me stop and think. They suggest movement. Jesus came to dinner, but he didn't stay on and on like some guests. Suddenly he was gone. And as I look over the accounts of the events clustered around Easter I get a distinct feeling of movement. All the records tell of someone on the move. I don't know how to explain it. Nor did they. Twelve men lock themselves inside a room, and they say that suddenly they were all aware of his presence. He speaks a word of peace and is gone. Others report seeing him here and then over yonder, first in one form and then another. And I get the feeling that someone had not come to stay put but to show us the way.

All at once I realize how seldom I have expected to meet Jesus anywhere except in the pages of a compact but far-ranging little black book with gold lettering. He does speak to me there, of course. But sometimes my struggle for meaning and value remain unsatisfied by simply looking to the Jesus of Nazareth who lived two thousand years ago. Why? Because while I bury myself in records of the past, Jesus Christ moves on! How slowly it dawns on me that he continues to appear, first here and then there, first in this form and then in that, as he moves on. And if any of this is true, then I have to admit that I often have the same trouble the first disciples had. They usually failed to recognize Christ when he appeared. And so do I. Mary desperately wanted to find Jesus. She went back to the tomb. But when he appeared to her she mistook him for the gardener. She simply did not conceive that he could be alive like that in the world still. Those two men on their way to Emmaus should have known Jesus at a glance. But somehow, after the bottom had dropped out of everything they didn't expect him to be walking their way again. Peter went fishing.

He didn't catch anything. Nor did he recognize Jesus standing on the beach. Peter just didn't assume Christ would be that interested any more in his job.

Now if Jesus is alive and still on the move in my world, I want to be on the lookout for him. I imagine that he will still appear in unexpected ways with the same kind of disturbing, life-changing word. Frankly, I sometimes wish he'd let things alone awhile. Some of the changes taking place in the world and in my own heart scare me. Still he keeps appearing and letting me know that if I think getting my own way will warm my heart, I'd better think again. Sometimes I feel as though someone had yanked all my old values right out from under me. But suppose Christ himself has a hand in that? If he does, then I have to decide whether I'm going to stand pat or get moving with God. And honestly, it isn't easy for me to make that choice. It isn't easy to embrace the new without losing the essential truth of things I have experienced in the past. It's a little scary to think that in mid-career I may have to be continually at the job of reshaping and restyling my whole life. I feel so vulnerable when I have to admit that many of my past assumptions are simply no longer viable. But I feel Christ continually asking me to decide whether or not I really want to participate with God in this century. How then can I know the truth that will set me free amongst the variety of these new experiences?

I seem to hear Jesus saying, "Art, do you know who the really fortunate people are? They're the ones whom life has pushed to the end of themselves. They come to a place where they realize that they cannot cope. It's often a place full of conflict and anguish. But at that place they throw themselves on God for safety and healing. The power to control their lives passes from their hands to His. And when that transfer takes place the world has one less candidate for misery. Such people no longer live at the mercy of circumstances. They begin to live by the mercy of God, and a deep inner healing begins.

And I say, "Right on, Lord, but in what places shall I look for you? If you're still on the move in my world, where can I look for your footprints in the events of my time?" And all at once I think I can begin to see his footprints in all efforts to relieve human suffering and restore human dignity. There's light on the horizon. You can't stop springtime when it starts to come.

And I begin to see how the new humanity offered me in Christ includes my body and my soul. After he died, the soul of Jesus did not go marching bravely on into some vague spiritual immortality. "They laid him in a grave, but God raised him. . . ." If that's true at all then God means to save me, body and soul. One's as sacred as the other. So in my world I see God on the move in Christ, in all efforts to feed people and to heal them. I also see Him in legislative efforts to insure human dignity and equal opportunity and to stop war and bring peace. I see Him on the move to renew those institutions that serve and support life and dignity.

One time Jesus turned to his disciples and said, "Don't you care about people? Give them something to eat." And like any good church committee they answered, "Lord, where can we get enough money to feed so many people?"

"Well," said Jesus, "just give them what you have, that's all!"

Some time later he told a story about how he will continue to come to me in the events and issues of my time. His story had to do with the end of time. Jesus described a scene where people stand before God. And he said that the Lord will say to some people, "You did a great job. Well done! Welcome to the joy of your Lord!"

That surprises them. They say, "Lord, what did we ever do for you that you should invite us to share your joy? When did we ever see you in trouble or hungry or without a house or in jail, and help you?"

And the Lord says, "Whenever you did any one of these things for the poorest man on earth you did it to me. Welcome, friend."

Then some other people come along and say, "Lord, we haven't heard our names yet. Aren't we on the list?"

And the Lord answers, "I beg your pardon, I don't think we've met. Who are you?"

"Well, Lord, we're your followers, too. But frankly, Lord, we never noticed you in jail, or going hungry, or without a place to stay. If we'd seen you, of course we'd have done something about it."

"Didn't you ever see me?" asks the Lord. "Well, let me tell you something. Whenever you refused to help one of the poorest ones on earth, you refused me."

And that is how and where Jesus appears amongst us today! In those unexpected and surprising places. That is where I can look for him in the events of my time. I begin to see him first in one place and then in another, and sometimes in both places at once. Just as after the first Easter. And he doesn't always look as I expect he might. Still I begin to reunderstand what it means to have an incarnation religion. It means that God keeps coming to me in the flesh as well as in the Spirit. He's alive and loose in the world like that. He does not answer all my questions, but he does go before me. The whole world looked like winter once, when I started out for Emmaus just to get away from it all. "They laid him in a grave, but God raised him. . . ." Now the sun is out and the air is full of life. You can't stop springtime when it starts to come.

And sometimes I think I can hear the Lord saying to me, "Art, the past does affect you. Your own personal past affects you, and so do certain watershed events in human history. You should take a good look at what has gone on inside of you and around you in your past. But then you should look beyond yourself. Look back through the years to what happened on Good Friday, see what the records say about it and about the resurrection. Look at me with your own eyes. As if you were seeing me for the first time. Forget for a minute all that the theologians have told you, and try to see me for yourself. But then, for God's sake, get moving! Don't stand there simply looking back into the past. Move on from a new seeing of the basic facts of the Christian faith to a more mature understanding of their significance for your life and time. Follow me. You'll always find me out in front of you. How could you possibly follow me if I remained forever behind you in the past? We don't need to go over and over again such elementary topics as 'Faith in God,' or 'The Doctrine of Baptism,' or 'Belief in the Life to Come,' or 'The Second Coming.' Let's move on!

"Let me show you the Father. He's forever making all things new. Yes, you'll see ugliness and tragedy all around you. But don't miss seeing the coming of God's springtime and those green shoots of new life poking their way up through the garbage. Follow me, and I'll show you that there's a future. I'm not leading you toward a dead end. Don't confuse God's kingdom with your idea of civilization. Civilization as you know it may indeed come to an end. Lots of civilizations have, and yours may. But I'm asking you to follow me to a world that will never end. A world God has had in mind and on His heart from the beginning. And I have a place for you in it, and important work for you to do. So come stand with me against the darkness and watch the light come."

NOTES

CHAPTER 1

1. G. A. Studdert Kennedy, *The Unutterable Beauty* (London: Hodder & Stoughton, 1927), p. 14.

CHAPTER 2

1. Clarence Jordan, *Sermon on the Mount* (Valley Forge, Pa.: Judson Press, 1970), pp. 93–96.

CHAPTER 3

1. Peter and Brigitte Berger, "The Blueing of America," *Theology Today*, July, 1971, pp. 216–18.
2. James D. Smart, *The Quiet Revolution* (Philadelphia: Westminster Press, 1969), p. 155.

CHAPTER 4

1. Albert Camus, *Resistance, Rebellion and Death*, trans. Justin O'Brien (New York: Alfred Knopf, 1961), p. 71.
2. John A. Mackay, *Christian Reality and Appearance* (Richmond: John Knox Press, 1969), pp. 88–89.

CHAPTER 5

1. Smart, *The Quiet Revolution*, pp. 56–70.

CHAPTER 6

1. Welch H. Alden, "Jesus was a Racist," *Pulpit Digest* (February 1972), pp. 10–12.
2. David Woodward, *To Be Human Now* (Philadelphia: Westminster Press, 1969), p. 78.

CHAPTER 7

1. Katherine Anne Porter, *Ship of Fools* (Boston: Little, Brown & Co., 1962), p. 145.
2. Benjamin Garrison, *Creeds in Conflict* (Nashville: Abingdon Press, 1967), p. 95.

CHAPTER 8

1. John A. Redhead, *Sermons on Biblical Characters* (Nashville: Abingdon Press, 1963), p. 112.
2. From an unpublished sermon of Theodore Parker Ferris preached in the fall of 1970.

CHAPTER 10

1. From an unpublished sermon of Theodore Parker Ferris.